THIRD EYE & KUNDALINI AWAKENING FOR BEGINNERS:

Guided Mindfulness Meditations, Yoga, Hypnosis & Spiritual Awakening Practices

Heal Your Chakra's & Energy, Psychic Abilities & More!

© Copyright 2021 - All rights reserved.

The content contained within this book may not be reproduced, duplicated or transmitted without direct written permission from the author or the publisher.
Under no circumstances will any blame or legal responsibility be held against the publisher, or author, for any damages, reparation, or monetary loss due to the information contained within this book; either directly or indirectly.

Legal Notice:
This book is copyright protected. This book is only for personal use. You cannot amend, distribute, sell, use, quote or paraphrase any part, or the content within this book, without the consent of the author or publisher.

Disclaimer Notice:
Please note the information contained within this document is for educational and entertainment purposes only. All effort has been executed to present accurate, up to date, and reliable, complete information. No warranties of any kind are declared or implied. Readers acknowledge that the author is not engaging in the rendering of legal, financial, medical or professional advice.

TABLE OF CONTENTS

INTRODUCTION ON HOW TO USE THIS BOOK 8

What You Will Get From Reading This Book & Thoughts To Consider Before Beginning 10

A Beginners Perspective On Spiritual Awakening Practices... 14

The Reality of Opening The Third Eye & Awakening The Kundalini 17

SECTION 1: A BEGINNERS INTRODUCTION TO AWAKENING THE KUNDALINI 19

CHAPTER ONE   The Third Eye, Pineal & Pituitary Glands 20

The Importance 22

Questions, Concerns and Insights Seekers Have: Clues To Know You're Ready 26

CHAPTER TWO What is The Kundalini? 30

What It Means To Be Awakened 37

Ancient Teachings 40

Dispelling Common Myths 45

SECTION 2: PREPARING FOR THE JOURNEY 48

CHAPTER THREE The 7 Chakra's, Location, Tools & How They Influence Your Life 49

The First Chakra– The Root Chakra 51

The Second Chakra– Sacral Chakra 58

The Third Chakra– Solar Plexus 64

The Fourth Chakra– The Heart Chakra 69

The Fifth Chakra– The Throat Chakra 76

The Six Chakra– The Third Eye.......................... 81

The Seventh Chakra– The Crown Chakra 88

CHAPTER FOUR Creating Space For The Practices of Awakening.. 93

Your Sleeping Practice 96

Your Kitchen: Treating Food as Medicine........ 102

Tapping Into The Senses 104

Using Intuition-Let Food Choose You 105

When Food Opens You Up 108

How You Store Your Food Matters.................. 111

How You Display Your Food Matters.............. 116

Herbs & Spices As Medicine 117

High Vibrational Home & Cleansing Practices 120

Scents, Herbs, & Resins That Clarify Your Space 124

CHAPTER FIVE   Additional Tools For Increased Results.. 133

Journaling & The Questions That Lead To Realization 135

The Questions That Lead To Realization 138

Music: Keeping Your Vibration High With Harmony 141

Nature's Contributing Factor 143

Community Participation & Support Groups . 145

CHAPTER SIX The Physical Journey to Awakening: Yoga 147

The Oldest Writings on Yoga 148

The Many Lineages Of Yoga 149

Beginners Methods to Open The Body & Mind 158

Making Yoga Simple & How To Develop A Practice 160

CHAPTER SEVEN Opening The Path To Liberation: Mindfulness Meditation 164

Identifying Mindfulness Meditation 166

Misconceptions 168

How To Develop A Practice That's Right For You 169

CHAPTER EIGHT Rewiring the Brain: Hypnosis . 171

What Is Hypnosis & What Are The Benefits? . 171

Reprogramming Your Mental Process 175

Example Of A Self-Hypnosis Practice: 179

CHAPTER NINE Healing & Experience 181

What Does Spiritual Healing Look Like? 183

Symptoms Of Chakra Healing 188

Interacting With Family & Friends While On Your Journey 203

Professional Therapists & Counselors As Helpful Resources 207

Professional Healers That Can Help 209

CHAPTER TEN The Gifs of Awakening 212

Increase Abilities & Enhance Senses 213

Psychic Abilities 214

The Clairsenses 215

How To Integrate The New You 221

CHAPTER ELEVEN Conclusion & Aftercare 225

Good Practices To Follow When Doing Spiritual Work 225

Recommendations For Staying Mentally Healthy 227

Using Meditation 228

Using Visualization To Manifest Your Future Desires 229

Music: Keeping Your Vibration High With Harmony 231

Conclusion & Where To Go From Here 232

SECTION 4: GUIDED MEDITATIONS FOR YOUR PATH 234

BONUS MEDITATIONS & AFFIRMATIONS 254

INTRODUCTION ON HOW TO USE THIS BOOK

Welcome to a new and exciting journey to your higher self! It is no accident that you have arrived at this moment in your life, you are ready to listen to the next steps of evolution. This book is to first be used as a text of information, a step by step process to open yourself and your heart so that you may obtain the opening of your Third Eye sight and Awaken the Kundalini present within you.

Secondly, this is to be served as a manual, one you feel inclined to come back to and study. Giving ourselves many chances to absorb the importance of this journey is of great benefit and will serve you well. You will have the chance to touch on lively practices that brings sustenance to where you lay your head at night and the place you receive your food. You will be offered the chance to break free and clarify new goals to live intentionally and fully connected to the 5-Senses (Taste, Touch, Smell, Hear, Speech).

You may feel inclined to go to particular sections to devour the information that feels pertinent to your mental fascination, but you are encouraged to follow a methodical approach. When you fully understand the back story–the why to a process, you not only have the opportunity to make better informed decisions, but the steps to achieve with greater ease.

This is an ancient connection to the lineages before us, the tribes, the medicine people, the Shaman, and Yogi's we have descended from. As you Awaken the slumbering inner workings of yourself, you will realize you have more magic, manifestation, and abilities that come to your mind. You may suddenly realize you have a connection to the occult, number patterns (Numerology), intuitive practices such as Tarot and Physic Vision. Nurture what comes up as you explore the words within this text. Listen to the callings of music, nature, and connecting with the animal spirits on this earth–it extensively links you to the old codes of harmony and divine order.

May you be blessed on this journey towards an Awakened future and be a guiding light for all you come across. Please hold your hands over your heart and repeat: May I be protected through my journey, may I hear the calling of my ancestors, may I awaken to my true self, and love who I am unconditionally. And so it is.

What You Will Get From Reading This Book & Thoughts To Consider Before Beginning

This book is to offer you a vast array of knowledge about the sensitive inner workings of your being, take care to be in safe places while taking in this important information, the frequency and absorption will have larger and more positive affect.

You will gain or "remember" ancient intelligence that is a part of who you are combined with the energy and frequency that your body is made up of. This is a step-by-step approach to Awakening the Kundalini through developing simple, yet effective practices to open the Third Eye and dive deeper into the depths of who you are.

It is recommended that you consider some important factors before moving forward, as this journey is one that blossoms with each passing day. The subtleties culminate to the larger picture of change, its truly being awake to the greater purpose of your presence in this magnificent time in our rapid changing history.

Are you ready to embark on a fun and challenging adventure to another side of yourself?

Some parts of you will be re-awakened, childlike intentions, memories good/bad, dreams and aspirations of the past may resurface.

Are you be willing to shift and move to accommodate your life with new habits?

Having a private space where you can naturally work on your new process is very important—even a closet will do. Consider if you are available to make small changes necessary to get where you want to be.

Are you prepared to have the way you are perceived by others to change?

Many people will have comments about who you are after some months of working with your bodies energy system. They many not all be as positive reviews as one would hope. Questions may arise that make you feel uncomfortable because you will be noticed in ways you weren't before. As you come into yourself more, you feel at ease being noticed for the easy ways you're able to master your life.

Are you ready for the time of your life?

When you are awakened again from a long slumber, you start to notice the small synchronistic events as they pop up in your awareness more each day. Following the practices outlined in this book will guide you to practices that give gratitude to these "coincidences"– we more correctly define as synchronicity. It makes you even more aware to gauge the best routes to take, the best foods to eat, and when to reach for a positive connection with another person.

Are you ready to emotionally level up?
Emotional maturity increases with this work as you put in the effort to discover your own emotional process. It includes your part in relationships whether it be work, romantic, friendship or familial—you'll begin to notice the dynamic will start to shift. The inclination to take responsibility regardless if you are right or wrong is the ultimate frame of mind is true freedom at heart. It an important aim of awakening the Kundalini. In turn, this process offers a chance to open up for genuine interactions, deeper love connections and understanding with people you want in your life.

Are you ready to redefine your relationships?
When you listen to the inner callings of safe and healthy relationships, you understand where your participation begins and where other persons participation ends. The approach is to get comfortable clarifying what you hope to establish with these relationships and together devise a way to refine the way you approach one another. When we create a safe space, when we come with a responsible nature and even disposition, we connect deeply to the people we come in contact with. Reception is a likely reaction as you approach the situation with hopes of reach a healthy

conclusion— it can be seen as an act of healing and moving forward.

Do you desire to rewire you mental tapes?
Has anyone ever told you that you are not the voice inside your head? As you navigate through the pages of this book, you will start to see how often you speak to yourself, you will start to identify its effect on your body and learn how to redirect that speech towards greater love and appreciation for yourself and those you surround yourself with. Letting go of mental tapes is an arduous task that takes many years to reprogram.

The practices in this book offer solid ways to help your mind release the unwanted thoughts of the future, memories of the past and what you think needs to completed right now. These will be honest attempts to reduce depression, anxiety and feelings of uneasiness in the body.

A Beginners Perspective On Spiritual Awakening Practices

A misconception with Spiritual Awakening is that everything becomes rosy in our lives, we no longer experience pain, we are master meditators and removed from conflict. This is not what Awakening brings even though these experiences occur much more often and for longer periods of time.

What is to be obtained is a sense of what it feels like to physically and mentally understand the concept of how to Awaken parts of yourself. To know what part of the body it is when someone mentions that their Solar Plexus seems blocked and to know the remedy to loosen the knots and get back to a state of equilibrium.

Spiritual Awakening is being equipped to deal with parts of life that seem difficult and hard to surpass. It's having a toolbox full of remedies that soothe, heal, and give strength to your inner being. It is a close connection to the subtle parts of life that stack on top of each other—making life feel beautiful in all of its quirky imperfections.

Below are a few things you may notice more right out the gate and you are encouraged to milk them for as long as you can—make the moment last.

-Birds singing, insects moving, and lustrous cloud formations in the sky. You are encouraged to look up anytime you have the chance to be outside.

-Interactions with people are so pleasant— the sweeter you are, the better the conversation. You leave better than when you arrived.

-Things you have been desiring start to show themselves again and opportunities to obtain them are closer within reach.

-You start to see your thoughts in books you read, podcast's you listen to, and conversations you overhear.

-People reaching out to you that have been on your mind or vice versa.

-Patience creeps upon you, realizing that the longer you wait, the more financially accessible it becomes.

-Overall pride of who you are and where you have come from.

-Encounters with certain people become noticeable— do they feed your spirit or bring you to a place you didn't want to be?

What to remember is there is no end goal to this process, it's a lifelong journey from here on out, and your experience will look different than those you see on Youtube or read on Blog posts. You are greatly encouraged to not compare yourself to others as it only complicates the situation and assigns feelings that don't serve your newly developed self.

Perfection or the right "look" should not be the focus because the more imperfect we are at something gives us the gift of true experience— its not a contest on who does it best. If you see behaviors or read about others that exude this, stay far away, it will not serve you.

The intention of this book is to connect you to knowledge that sits dormant inside your bodies design and as you open up you'll realize you have much more inside that needs self expression— stumbling on talents and hobbies you have long forgotten or didn't even know was a passion come back once again. In no way is this book to serve over your internal guidance system and intuition, nor take the place of your prescribed therapies. Please listen to yourself and only begin another section when you feel comfortable with where you are.

The Reality of Opening The Third Eye & Awakening The Kundalini

The reality of this journey is that it isn't exactly an easy feat. You can do all of the practices, but if you are not internally ready to see something different for yourself, then you may have a tumultuous time as the energies you awaken push you towards breaking free of stagnation. You will come to know that any discomfort or unease is yet another part of yourself looking for release.

You may look up other peoples experiences to realize they have had a violent or terrible time discovering parts of their psyche because they didn't have a language to identify their experience, they did not have access to, or know of the remedies to soothe themselves through the encounters and to the beauty on the other side. This does not have to be your process and don't be turned off by the negative experiences of others while they go through the same types of challenges. We all have deep wounds we are working with.

It took you many years to become the person you are today and to unwind some of that will take many years to refine, but that's the beauty–there is no end to this journey once you begin. You may also be surprised to realize that some parts of your life will dismantle quickly, the moment to upgrade has been waiting at the gate for you. As you close many doors, others will quickly open, leading you to better versions of your daily experience.

While exciting new experiences lay on the other sides of newly opened doors you can imagine the types of challenging scenarios that may come up. It can include the loss/quitting of a job for something you've always wanted, but was afraid to reach for. It can be that relationship that has been shifting and possibly separating because the goals are no longer aligned. You may be inclined to finally start talking to that person you've avoided for years and finally attain a sense of closure. You can suddenly desire to share more of what you have or take back what you have given too freely. Ultimately you gain a sense of power over your experience, but its not to be obtained without some types of pain, uncertainty, or discomforts.

Another reality with this journey is to be willing to change the script so to speak. Before starting the careful process of Awakening yourself to the Kundalini and Third Eye sight you may have had grandiose plans that fit the person that stands here today, but realize this person will become more refined. The ease of life you wish to obtain will become more accessible as you let go of planned situations as you evolve—as you grow, so will your dreams and desires.

SECTION 1: A BEGINNERS INTRODUCTION TO AWAKENING THE KUNDALINI

CHAPTER ONE
The Third Eye, Pineal & Pituitary Glands

We will get into the depths of the Third Eye and how to work with it in Chapter 3, here we will discuss the concept of what it is and how it intertwines with normal functions and actual body parts and organs within the body. The Third Eye is not some New Age fad word about being "woke". It directly linked with your intuitive sense of sight. Its how you stay out of danger, avoid pitfalls, and make a left because it seemed safer when in actuality, you should have turned right. The Third Eye is a representation of having the foresight to make decisions that best suit your cosmology.

Your Third Eye is the sight within the dream state that is remembered when we awaken, it's the feeling of tension between the brow when you don't understand, or a tingling sensation when you eat fresh, pure, juices, foods, or smoothie's. It's the reminder to stay aware, observe your surroundings carefully and know when to adapt if necessary. It is a sight between the eyes that we may not normally sense with the two we read with, however there are people who do which is called Clairsentience and a part of the Psychic or Clairsenses people experience as a result to being open to seeing beyond what others term "reality". We will discuss the Clair's more carefully in Chapter 10.

The Pineal Gland operates the glandular system located between the hemispheres of our brain and is responsible for secreting Melatonin. Melatonin is what helps regulate the sleep and wake cycles of our life—our circadian rhythm. Its renowned as being responsible for our extra sensory awareness and what some constitute as ultimate enlightenment. Over time with improper eating and consumption of toxic beverages, age, and disease, calcification begins to take place.

Other traditions that talk about the Awakening of the Kundalini talk about the Pituitary gland being the central location for keeping the bodies balance and rhythm aligned. The Pituitary glad is the gland of all glands and is the central gate keeper for the functionality and performance of the glandular system. Because this gland would control the Pineal, some say this would be the superior gland to assign to the Third Eye, but it is up for debate because each experience is different. How do you know which one is activated if you've never tried it for yourself? And if all of these Yogis and practitioners know the organs, how could one be wrong and the other be correct? The Third Eye allows us the sight to see that it doesn't matter much, what matters is the practice and attainment of reaching awakening or enjoying the activation of the Chakra system.

The Importance

Both of these areas of the head combined spell a message that's loud and clear–connection to your natural rhythm is essential for getting closer to your purpose in life. You ultimately clarify your vision and it works to keep you on track to continue your daily practices so you obtain your ultimate goals. A vast amount of people have upset sleeping patterns, the muscles are unable to fully relax and the mind races with all the thoughts of lack, responsibilities and endless to-do lists. Poor posture, the wrong pillow, or the wrong temperature in your room can also lead to nights of tossing and turning. This ripples to your circadian rhythm (natural time cycle) aiding in your 3pm crash, midnight social media binges to "get sleepy" or needing the TV on to fall deeply asleep. While we all suffer from these temptations and issues, the good news is there are ways to improve–not to perfect, but to increase energy to continue on, improving day by day, small incremental steps towards happiness. More to come on the subject of sleep in Chapter Four.

These subjects are implemented in a chapter of its own for you to connect to the inner and outer workings of verbiage people use to describe an ultimate state of being by Awakening the Kundalini and Opening the Third Eye.

Why would a Third Eye be closed? It's not necessarily closed and needs to be open but is a metaphorical concept for being unaware of the larger themes of life– what is actually attained is activation. It is when people are unable to see the bigger reasons for the experience they are having and have the inability to see it in another light. When a Third Eye is open/Awakened a person takes direct responsibility for the knowledge the consume, the people they take information from, and the transformation of patterns that no longer bring joy, light, harmony and peace. The closure however is a true concept for what it should actually look like, an eye closed and focused on the inner workings of the subject.

When you open/Awaken your Third Eye, it is because you have unlocked and continue to work with the other energies of your Chakra system. The Third Eye is the Sixth Chakra out of 7, it is the second from the last to attain "enlightenment" or complete and utter bliss. When we work diligently with the areas of our body represented by the Chakra's, we understand how connected we are internally. We can see clearly how our thoughts located in the area of the Third Eye, the center of the eyebrows–the brain– controls how our belly feels (3rd Chakra: Solar

Plexus) and how it intertwines with our anxiety and rapid heart beat (4th Chakra: The heart). The things you are learning are real and wholly connected to the cosmos and everything around you.

Now that you understand the importance, you may be harboring many questions as to if you have an open Third Eye, if you can purify your Pineal Gland for better sleep patterns and if you are ready to embark upon the journey then the answer is, YES!

You've chosen this book to dive deeper into yourself, to shift your beliefs, and achieve an overall sense of happiness by participating in ancient practices that help you feel wellness at a deep level. When you open your mind by taking in information led by your intuitive guidance you see so much more value than if you weren't ready. In fact, if you weren't ready, you wouldn't have been searching for a title such as this. Welcome back to the remembering of your inner knowledge.

Below is a list of phrases, questions, concerns and wonderment about life that people just like you ask on a daily basis that are ready to take a leap of faith. Opening your Third Eye and Awakening your Kundalini is a slow and steady approach to increasing your awareness and finding the drive and motivations that make you excited about living each day to the fullest. What's important to note is that you can be at any state of your evolution to delve into the inner workings of the Kundalini and its connection to the higher planes of the instinctual, yet physical parts of the body.

Questions, Concerns and Insights Seekers Have: Clues To Know You're Ready

What is the purpose of my life?
Should I have a bigger impact on the world?
I am sick of this (fill in the blank) happening to me, how do I detach from it?
I need something more to connect to.
I need spirituality in my life.
I want to know more about practices I connect to.
Do I have the authority to explore the Third Eye and the Kundalini on my own?
I don't feel scared by what could happen, I am excited by the endless possibility.
I am looking for more out of life.
People tell me I am "connected", but I am not sure how.
I want to learn how to live a better life on my own.
I am open to any and all practices of the world as long as they have moral value and spirit.
I enjoy topics on metaphysics.
I have studied or know about NLP (Neurolinguistic programming).
I want to learn more about Hypnotherapy.
I practice Yoga and want to learn about the deeper concepts of why I do it.
I enjoy self improvement, but I am looking for something deeper.

I am coming out of a state of depression and looking for hope.
I am a beginner and I just want to learn the concepts.
I am a novice and I'd like another point of view.
The worlds disasters has me wondering if there is anything more.
I am blessed to be alive from the worlds Pandemic and desire devotion to my new lease on life.
I have survived traumatic events in my life and am ready to safely move on.
I see a therapist or counselor and they have encouraged me to explore self study.
I am a therapist and want to understand the people who speak about this in my presence.
I am a counselor and I want to better know the person I am helping who does these practices.
I am a forever student and desire to learn more.
How do I take my power back?
How do I become a medicine person?
I want to help people in the world, but I don't know what it should be.
How do I increase my intuitive abilities?
How do I get my feet wet with Meditation?
I'm not flexible, so I don't do Yoga.
I want to heal from a bad relationship.
I want to know more about the Chakra system.
People always talk about Meditating, but I don't like it.
Meditation doesn't work for me.
How do I improve my relationships?

How do I improve my mental state?
Do I have special abilities I am not aware of?
I am doing all the things but nothing seems to be working.
There is something missing from my daily practice, but I don't know what it is.
Im tired of hearing this New Age lingo, what is it exactly?
I am a private person and I don't want to take a class to learn the basics.
I am a self starter and need something with substance.
How can I interlink all my practices?
Do I have to choose just one practice or can I try them all?
I am interested in Astrology and Tarot.
I approach life with a holistic point of view.
I have the power to change my life and my circumstances.
I see colors, shapes and visions when I close my eyes in Meditation.
I enjoy contemplation.
I am ready for life's new possibilities.
I am a Yoga teacher expanding my personal practice.
I work really hard and need something to relax me.
I am unemployed and looking to expand my mind while I discover what my next path is.
I want to start a business, but I feel unconnected to what it should be centered around.

I am an Entrepreneur and looking to add value to my daily life.

I employ a large number of people with differing beliefs who are young and seekers of knowledge.

I want to connect with fun loving people who have diverse beliefs.

I am looking to increase my arsenal of tools.

I now work from home and desire peace back in my home.

I want to escape.

I feel helpless at the moment, how do I move forward?

My social media feeds wont stop recommending this stuff to me.

All of my quirky but interesting friends are into this stuff, what's the hype?

Is this some New Age fad that will pass with time?

The list of questions can proceed for many pages, the point is to prove that you can be in any stage of life, age, or experience to be ready for this information and eye opening journey. This Chapter we have covered the importance of the Third Eye, the Pineal & Pituitary Glands, and how to know if you are in the right mental space to do this work. In the next chapter we will dive deeper into the main essence of the Kundalini and the larger purpose and inner workings of its Awakening process.

CHAPTER TWO
What is The Kundalini?

The Kundalini is the seed and the essence of who you are, the truest and highest form of knowing the Self. When we talk about the Kundalini, we are talking about an infinite energy that cannot be measured in size, but rather the large implications it brings to your life's awareness. It is represented by the energy of Shakti moving up the body to join with Shiva– two ancient gods in the Hindu tradition that long to be together as one.

Shiva and Shakti are the representation of the divine union of Energy and Consciousness. Shiva is the masculine representation of a person achieving consciousness. Shakti is the feminine creating the energy it takes to get to ultimate liberation and union with consciousness– the place where our natural state of bliss resides.

The Kundalini Shakti lays dormant at the base of the spine, split in two, helping us deal with the mundane parts of life and once awakened, enlivens every sense of who we know ourselves to be. Waking up the senses is one of the first initiations into its vast technology. When a person is waking up to their life they wake up in a state of quite, then, hopefully satisfaction, for another day is upon you! The days where you wake up, look at the ceiling and realize who and where you are with disdain will start to slowly diminish as the beauty of life starts to make its self known and more accessible.

The 5-senses are always the first indication that things are changing for you—this is the unraveling of the Kundalini. Your sight may improve as you continue down the Yogic path utilizing its many Kriya''s (Yogic exercises) to strengthen sensitive parts of the eye that diminish through heavy use of computers, smart phones, and overbearing lights. You may notice you see things out of the corner of your eye that possibly scare you, or make you wonder what you possibly saw or what you were thinking about that would manifest a vision. What occurs under the eyelids could be described as your own cosmic symphony—many people manifest different visions based on their life experiences and what serves them best at that time. People report seeing vivid colors swirling and jumping in front of a black lit back drop. Other report illuminating visions of people they love, places they wish to visit or the solar system as it moves though its cycles.

The Kundalini awakens the sight inwardly and enlivens the life outwardly by giving a sense of foresight that exceeds natural planning, lists, and goal sets. This is knowing when you see something of value and following your instincts. Say you turn off the highway onto a dirt road hoping to find a place to rest your head, only to realize you don't know where you are and only have a half tank of gas. You would sleep in your car if you could only find a safe place to park, then off in the distance many tiny lights show up ahead, wow only a few miles in and something is starting to surface. When you pull up it's a large habitat to your right and many bustling busy people enjoying their stay– you have arrived. Not only did you turn off the road in perfect timing, but you trusted in something higher to get you there. Now not only do you get a good nights rest feeling safe amongst people like you, it was free and only a few miles off the main road. This is the Kundalini's magic, it is they way events are aligned for the perfect moment in time.

The Kundalini awakens the taste buds, creating a refinement and appreciation for the location, love and ingredients harvested. Its understanding where the food you eat comes from and the importance of the highest quality foods we can afford and have access to. It starts to help simplify the pallet, not for lack of taste, but giving more focus to fresh foods and spices that were carefully chosen to begin the base of an amazing meal. The Kundalini will remind us of ancient grains, herbs, tinctures, extracts and oils that add dimension and depth to a meal. Its sitting back after a meal, completely satisfied with the combination of sweet, salt, sour, and bitter flavors that give satisfaction to all the sections of the tongue. Its making a meal a sensual experience of high quality and visual beauty that makes you feel fortunate for what you have.

Its as simple as taking a trip to the market and buying as many things as you can make from scratch or even buying your favorite cheese or hot sauce to compliment what you make. The idea is to engulf your plate or bowl with foods that bring you joy and a sense of feeling "full". Full of love, full of life and could even go for a nice brisk walk, not too full to move. Its stopping by the neighbors apartment a few blocks down to gather a few of her window sill grown dill and oregano or once a week treating yourself to a fruit plate or fresh baked bread you adore. You don't have to become a person that spends too much money on food to make it count and this includes those that live in food deserts (places where grocery stores are obsolete). Your local bodega down the street can become an ally for you if you reach out and ask for something more—there is always a way, even if its small.

The Kundalini awakens the sense of touch so you notice the subtle breezes, the tickle of small hairs, delicate skin creases, and sweat glands you didn't know you had. What magnificence that our bodies contain the grace of all these things at once. Its also connected to the enjoyment of a tender embrace, a handshake or a pat on the back from someone and noticing what their energy feels like. Do they feel positive, warm, soft, nervous, or sad? Touch is the technology of your muscles, skin, and brain receptors–feeling your way around to the most trusting and safe forms of touch you can find to increase happiness and overall sense of well-being.

The Kundalini begins to awaken more in terms of smell. What begins to happen is noticing the subtle scents of flowers, pine needles and jasmine blooming. Foods begin to taste differently because your sense of smell is heightened and driven to choose the most fragrant and appealing. You can walk through a store and smell the fresh cut flowers, seasoned meats, and freshly baked breads.

You also notice perfumes smell not so natural. You notice people mask the scent of their bodies because they are desensitized, dousing themselves in chemicals to have the appearance of top notch hygiene and self care. As you lesson the amount of fragrances you use on yourself, which is a natural progression of a blossoming Kundalini, you start to smell things you haven't smelled since you were a child. A breeze can go by and remind you of the sweetest smell of your grandma or old car your dad used to take you for a ride in. Capturing these moments make's life just a tad sweeter, lighter, and more quiet.

One of the most connecting forms of the Kundalini Awakening within you is the ability to carry out a conversation or emote your feelings in a concise and calm manner. There is a superpower in choosing your words wisely, deciding the best times to speak, and when you do, your ideas, power and self confidence show through. Its quite noticeable how your influence with words effects your experience and the world around you. Taking a step back now allows you to calculate and design the life of your dreams through speaking it into existence.

Have you ever been driving down the road and notice something you've wanted for a long time? Maybe it's a new car, beauty indulgence, or beautiful home and wonder to yourself— I've been driving down this road for a long time now, everyday, how come I didn't notice that before?— it's almost as if something you've wanted has been transplanted in real time reminding you of dreams and aspirations you once longed for. You then begin to see images resembling what you've seen everywhere you go, your friends are buying a new car and got a great deal while you've been waiting to buy one, or your co-worker had their hair done by a spectacular colorist and got you a card. Its these small alignments that help you to see what else you can manifest or bring to life that you desire. Go small, try foods first, getting a great parking spot, choosing the perfect time to avoid lines at the store, or going to the movies and seeing the next film playing at the slot you arrived at. See where life gives you a safe landing when you explore the dimensions of spontaneity, positive self talk, and creating small experiences with desirable outcomes.

However, don't be fooled, some events that occur often feel like a time of not being ready. You said you wanted a new job and two weeks later you have a friend that needs you for design work at a new firm, but you aren't ready, its not enough pay initially, or its halfway across the country. While seemingly inconvenient because comforts are being challenged, why would this time be as good as any to make a move? When you don't commit to your desires by fulfilling what you say you will, life has a way of forcing you to do it. While some may say its crazy to move far away from your friends and family to have the opportunity to work for a non-profit and help masses— you'll find yourself doing it anyways. Taking a risk starts to feel guided by divine intervention, safely placing you in environments that extend growth, wealth and more humble beginnings.

What It Means To Be Awakened

When beginning the journey, what it means to be awakened is what had decided to wake up inside of you. As delight for the next moments of experience arise, what do you feel passionate about? As you move from place to place or talk to random strangers about the weather, what about those moments brings you the most joy? Did you laugh, did you relate and connect deeply? What color were there eyes and who did they remind you of? As you see someone living their dream traveling the world on a school bus, how does it make you feel about where you are? Are you moved enough to change your situation so it looks more aligned with the vision in your head? Do you want a patio garden, to care for an animal, or spend more time with someone you love? These are all moments of awakening, bit by bit the onion of your life begins to peel and deeper parts of your awareness start to make themselves clear.

It can look like going back to school to learn about that subject your parents told you was useless, it can also be taking a Master-class for $40 because it helps you organize your closet better. Whatever it is, as long as its breaking through the barriers of original habits and routines that keep you in the same space, you are on track. Knowledge not only gives us the opportunity to make different choices in life, but it expands our beliefs to cover more ground, to include more people, and to accept more views. This becomes a softening of the heart and an understanding of compassion whether it was your direct experience, or a short film about a transgender teen, your exposure to learn lifts you to the higher echelons of life experience.

Awakening can come all at once for some people as some describe the experience to be shocking to the core after numerous pitfalls bring them to a place of surrender. The person often experiences a cataclysm like any other in their immediate life experience and they are knocked down to a place of complete humility and reverence for the process. Some talk about the physical sensations they experience which will be covered in Chapter Nine, that detail horrific rashes and erosions that show themselves when a person is actively clearing the way for more life to occur. While some paint it as an experience that is unbearable, some are able to notice what's leaving the body, and what will create space.

Support for these experiences may be necessary as some may feel a loss of control that is more than they are comfortable with— and that's okay. It's recommended for you to connect with others along the same journey by utilizing the vast array of App's and communities at our fingertips. Experiences that soothe your worry or feelings of loneliness in the process can be curbed until you feel settled.

Another great tool is discussing this process with a trusted friend and asking if you can divulge the journey, maybe not asking for advice, but a soundboard for the process unfolding inside of you. If you have no one in your life you are ready to trust or have issues with exposing yourself on social media, its recommended to continue the practices outlined in SECTION 3: THE PRACTICE AND THE JOURNEY.

Ancient Teachings

So what exactly does it mean to be Awakened? The Buddha and Zen masters agree that to be Awakened is to be Enlightened and to be Enlightened means to end all suffering of self for the chance of ultimate liberation. Liberation from the material, removal of attachment in outcomes, relationships, or day to day experiences that would normally cause a rise within us. However people tend to take this out of context, as the Buddha and masters alike knew these practices would benefit the householder, the person who serves their community, creates jobs, works for themselves, loves the corporations they hold positions in and people who stay home to care for family members and friends. It's the many ways of approaching how to get there and the many ways we can practice that give more benefit— the more people able to practice whole heartedly, the better.

Yogic teachings point to the Kundalini residing at the base of the spine coiled and asleep until its awakened to stand upright. As you attain higher frequencies of living, the snake or better called "serpent" rises through the body and the Chakra system to help give the practitioner a heightened sense of well being, challenge through breaking barriers of past patterning, and revealing a polished and refined individual. While this description is to be true for their lineage, a beginner can glean the importance of Chakra's, the Kundalini, the Third Eye, and somatic processes as attainment to the bigger picture of life. Its yet another lineage that believes in the process of lifting one's life through the process of letting go and getting to know the Self at a deeper capacity.

Two of the oldest traditions in the world believe there is a path to evolution and a liberation from what no longer serves the Self– what no longer extends the life-force. The Buddhist tradition reminds us that we are not our mind through Mindfulness Meditation and the Yogic teaching offers the bodily connection though moving the energy up the body with the use of physical movements and dynamic breathing. Both starting with a solid base either cross legged or standing straight in mountain pose, arms at side and legs strongly supporting each section of the body. It is here we hinge, move, gain stillness, begin the process, and birth new creations. It is important to remember the value of a stable lower body so there is a foundation you can rely on. While painful at first, sitting for 5 minuets or bending over may feel overwhelming and a point you cannot surpass, but with time and attention to the foundation it grows in strength, offering longer lengths of time sitting in peace or a full body bend that creates no tension in the lower back and thighs– baby steps coupled with child's mind, simple, yet effective.

Beginners Approach

Having a beginners approach to Awakening the Kundalini and opening your Third Eye is having a beginners mind. A beginners mind is an approach to leaving what you know behind and having a mind like a child– ready to absorb the new lessons that relate to the inner Self and newly adopted beliefs. When applying the methods you learn in this book it is important to remember your humble beginnings and look at people who aren't where you are as examples of what it looked like to be you at some point in the distant past. You will find the number of people interested in your journey or what you've been up to lately ramp up with inquisitive mentions about your glowing appearance, your outstanding performance, or immaculate organizational and preparation skill. This is the time we disclose small doses of our process, and you'll know who is actually interested and who is fishing for information– proceed with caution.

A great way to remain on track is to start small and build naturally. There may be the tendency to crave everything at once during a certain point in your evolution, wondering at a basic level when life will finally begin to look like you imagined and what you are striving for. This is the peak before it begins to plateau and will catapult you to the next level of the game. While the phrase "slow and steady wins the race" is cliche in nature, its safe to assume that its true and many scholars, gurus, wisdom keepers, and healers will attest to this journey for themselves. Wisdom is like fine wine, it only gets better with time.

The greatest tool to knowing everything is realizing that you know nothing– that is the greatest gift of opening your body and mind to Awakening. The more you research, the history you have been fed and the practices you no longer connect to began because you didn't know any different. Again you are in the process of knowing nothing until you start to awaken, absorbing, processing, digesting, and implementing a newly cultivated life– stepping deeper into the unknown as you turn over more stones of valuable truths you connect to internally. This is the mind of a child without being an adolescent, a cultured, experienced, emotionally mature person, open to new points of view with the willingness to expand to higher realms of thinking and belief patterns.

Ultimately the beginners approach is the best way to self knowledge and seeking for more– never becoming stagnant in your ability to usher small incremental changes to a more lively experience. Remaining in this process gives you a front row seat to the sideshow of know it all's and people that offer advice of no value. As you move through your journey you will discover people you can hear clearly and others whom you need a dictionary to understand or painfully watching them explain their process though a white board and it still feeling disconnected. While its important to keep your mind open to new and expansive points of view, its important to remember the certain centers of your body that serve as warning signals to better choices and guidance. Following your gut is an old adage, but relevant in any and every generation.

Dispelling Common Myths

Myths can turn into nasty little rumors that leave a bad taste in one's mouth, closing the door of opportunity and discovery. Here we would like to offer words of encouragement through times when you notice people talking about experiences they have heard or seen, but in actuality, have never experienced themselves. If your sisters, cousins, best friend had a bad experience meditating and blames all of their current issues on the Kundalini– they haven't found it and its okay to move on from their "experience" unbothered as you move through your own unique methods.

Myth: Awakening the Kundalini is a sexual practice.
Truth: Although it can enhance the experience or quell the overdrive of one's desire to have it, this is not a sexual based practice.

Myth: This process usually looks negative.
Truth: It's a positive experience towards learning about your inner workings and learning about your divine timing, willingness to laugh at yourself, and lessons for the why's and how's to your personal experience.

Myth: Awakening the Kundalini will ruin your life.
Truth: On the contrary it will break apart life as you now know it, but its not to ruin, it's to make ruin's

of the past trauma, hurt, anger, sadness and depression that plagues our beloved family members, whole communities, and nations torn apart by circumstance.

Myth: You will no longer need a therapist or counselor to talk to.
Truth: It is best to stay connected until the relationship is truly done.

Myth: You can and should remove all the "toxic" people from your life now that you have obtained an Awakened state.
Truth: It is better to work through the relationships you see as valuable and salvageable to sustain. Sometimes its just a matter of getting on the same page with one another.

Myth: You should remove yourself from any and all medications now that you understand yourself.
Truth: With anything, its best to listen to your medical doctor if you consult one and display the steps needed to witness your improvement. Allow them to recommend the safest approach to adapting your body to a new scenario.

Myth: You will go crazy or loose your mind studying this path.
Truth: Many gurus, yogis and ancient masters have chosen the path to enlightenment through the

study, practice and opening of the Kundalini Chakra's.

SECTION 2: PREPARING FOR THE JOURNEY

CHAPTER THREE
The 7 Chakra's, Location, Tools & How They Influence Your Life

The Kundalini is comprised of 7 main energy centers or knots within the body that contribute to the experience of Awakening the deepest parts of who you are. These knots can be represented as a swirling ball of energetic connections pulsing and reacting as you move through parts of your life. The ancient Yogic lineage of Kundalini Yoga describes the Chakra's as your God given gift to enlightening yourself and being a good steward to the place you inhabit, the people you love or are getting to know. A Chakra is interpreted to be a "wheel or disk" containing this energy of swirling energetic connectivity. It's a path that is not always linear, you may not experience it as an opening one Chakra at a time, but really a spontaneous Awakening where things start to make a lot more sense in the world. The lineage of Kundalini Yoga also cautions against forcing an awakening to happen through these practices, but instead understand the concepts, know the ideology, and to become a part of a larger community of people who too, are working on themselves.

Know this path is not to be taken alone. To be intellectually understood alone can be done quite well as the vocabulary and concepts imprint you for the longer journey ahead, but the full Awakening occurs when you thread yourself in a community of friends, trained Yoga teachers, Therapists, Counselors, Anthropologists, Teachers, activists, and the list goes on. Your experience can be relayed because any number of these people have experienced blockages or issues getting past points in their lives and have creative ways to solve some of them— we all work together to be a part of the change because we do better in numbers.

When the Kundalini is awakened through devotion, practice and concentration on the divine there is a realization of the greater lessons in why you are here, what you're meant to do in the world and the means with which you will get there. Awakening each area of the body is not something that is felt alone as a sensation, but instead initiates a way of being. When certain chakra's wake up from a long slumber and of having been pushed aside, they open up new ways of living that continue the influence of your daily practice.

The way you get to a Kundalini awakening is through the chakra's and taking the necessary steps to follow the path you are guided to walk on.

The chakra's comprise of a loop that starts from the base of the body while seated and moves the energy up the spine one chakra at a time. Through

Yogic practice, self study through this book, the help of people trained in Kundalini Yoga, chakra work, and energy healing puts you on a safe and healthy journey toward the path of ultimate happiness.

The First Chakra— The Root Chakra

Sanskrit Name: Mooladhara Chakra
Associated Color: Red
Body Location: The Base of the Seated Body (Anus)

The First chakra is the seed in which the plant begins to grow and take shape. It is where the serpent energy has coiled within each of us 3 and a half times, waiting for the chance to lengthen, grow, and help us transcend. The goal is to obtain a level of consciousness that drives the evolution of our life to progress and to move past the lower parts or energies of our lives. The First chakra is where everything begins, you cannot open the heart and have Third Eye vision without having Awakened this area of your body first.

The Sanskrit name for this chakra is called the Mooladhara, Moola means root and the foundation where everything lays upon it. It is when a student picks up a book, studies ancient text, develops a practice, and realizes they want more out of a relationship than just a sexual one. It is awakened though long times of abstinence and deep devotional practice towards saving the release of that bodily emotion by focusing on true connection.

The color red represents its animalistic value on your system, the instinctual parts of our psyche, why we rise, get angry, or want to fight. Red is the color of strength, war, the blood that runs through our veins and the signal we need to push the break peddle. It represents the fire inside that sends us on a journey to something new, burning away all that held us hostage.

This chakra stores all of our abuse, guilt, passions, desires and deep seeded fears. This is the chakra where we learn to control our sexual impulses to transcend to the next stage and evolve–one does not have to renounce it all together. The purpose is to utilize the energy of release when manifesting with another individual, when you both are on the same page connecting with the divine and each other simultaneously.

The location may make some scratch their heads, but it is actually different for the females then males. For the male parts, the Root is located at the perineum between the anus and sexual organ. For females this energy center lies in the area of the cervix. These are the areas responsible for childbirth, for arousing our deepest senses, it is our alert system when we feel fear and is the area that warms or scales up the spine when awakened. Some report being able to have extended sight through clairvoyance and heightened hearing through clairaudience. This is the chakra where some have out of body experiences, seeing themselves outside of their bodies during meditations, dreams and visualization. Both of these are a quiet whisper to be led on the next steps to move towards or ideas to investigate. Being mentally led or physically guided to new frames of reference and experience are likely to be a common theme when this chakra has received a release and opening of energy that is ready for the next steps of initiation.

When you are in your Root chakra, you are experiencing the lowest energies of human existence. While drugs, partying, casual sex and long nights out on the town feel invigorating and stimulating to participate in, this is where the Root sleeps. In high states of inconsistent behavior, practices and toxins the energy is not able to move to the next step. When you are full of negative thoughts of others and cant seem to catch a break, you can experience a sense of being stuck in the Root chakra.

Helpful Tool:
5 Crystals/Gems/Stones you can work with by holding, meditating with, visualizing on, or wear as

jewelry that assist with the subtle changes in the Root chakra:

Hematite-grounding and adds protection for out of body experiences. Dissolves negativity and balances out the Yin energy in the body by introducing more Yang. Enhances willpower and reliability. Can mentally stimulate concentration, memory, and focus. Hematite has the ability to bring your attention to unfulfilled desires that drive daily functions— helps with recognizing and correcting addictions.

Obsidian- helps raise the Kundalini, increases vitality and protection. Impels you to grow and learn. A stone that forces you to face up to your true self and taking you deep into the subconscious mind. Self control is increased with use. Repels negativity of others and disperses unloving thoughts and actions.

Smokey Quartz- energy amplifier, stores, releases and regulates energy while helping to unblock it. Connects the mental dimensions with the physical ones. Exposes blockages, weakness, and flaws as it is all truth enhancing. Aids in shadow work and spiritual integrity. A great stone to meditate with as it raises one's vibration. It helps dissolve contradictions and promotes concentration. Provides protection and connects one with the energies of the Earth.

Bloodstone- known as an audible oracle as it enhances sound, heightens intuition and assists in bringing spirituality into everyday life. Psychologically, Bloodstone can give the courage and teach how to avoid dangerous situations by strategically withdrawing and being flexible when needed. It aids in reducing irritability, aggressiveness and diplomacy towards others.

Black Tourmaline- connects you to the Root chakra, increases physical vitality and disperses tension and stress. Enhances overall states of well-being and heals the effects of psychic attacks. Promotes against electromagnetic smog, ill-wishing and aids in a more laid back approach. Neutrality and being clear are also effects of this stone.

To aid in the process of healing and allowing the energy to blossom, sitting in grassy or sandy areas (clothed) such as the park, the beach, an abandoned lot, a block of concrete, or a huge solid rock, will absorb the energy of the earth. It brings instant relief to menstrual cramps and overactive sexual sensations. This connection to the earth seats you upon the foundation you walk upon, grounding yourself and immersing your body with the natural rhythms of the earth.

This area of the body is mentioned to be an area of emotional upheaval. It is the place where greed, anger, stress, and jealousy lye within the body.

When this area is stimulated and increased sense of these emotions and feelings will arise and the tip is to remember that it occurs and to move through it. At the core these feelings stem from a sense of lack that either comes from having very little as a child or experiencing struggle at any point from adolescence to adulthood, which pretty much encompasses every human being. Lack can be experienced through a state of resources, not having enough attention and interest in one's life, or not getting the love desired and needed for emotional maturity. When you are in a constant state of survival or automatic movements in life, you forget that you have needs that need to be met because what fills the mind first are these mental tapes of lack and not being able to let go of the emotion attached.

Whether you suffer from food scarcity because you starved as a child, you too experience greed from a standpoint of survival, not because you don't want to or are unwilling to share what you have. Jealousy can come about when we see something we've wanted for some time become a part of someone else's reality and we want it. This again comes from a sense of lack, possibly because you never got what you wanted when you were a child, or you always felt like the odd man out because you weren't popular or worshiped by others in your youth. This is a learned behavior that can be broken as the mental tapes begin to be pulled out.

The Root chakra encompasses a lot of areas of life, but covers the most basic and the most mundane portions. When this Chakra is ready to be awakened the undesirable emotions listed above begin to agitate you, force you to take another look at the way you exist today and if it's the way you'd like to continue. Would you rather not be mad because someone cut you off in traffic and now you are not first? Would you rather look at someone and not wish you were that person or had the things they did because you are comfortable with yourself? These are questions and concerns a person will have when putting heat to the Root Chakra. Are you constantly worried about how others perceive or think about you? This is the place where you learn to leave those thoughts behind and start to focus inwardly on moving stagnated energy. While it takes years to not feel these emotions from time to time, the goal is to fundamentally understand when you are in that state and notice how it makes you feel. Your Awakened energy will assist you on the next moves to help heal.

The Second Chakra– Sacral Chakra

*Sanskrit Name: Swadhisthana Chakra
Associated Color: Orange
Body Location: Reproductive Organs*

The Second Ccakra is the place where one learns to own. This chakra is involved with the First chakra to aid in beginning to Awaken the whole system, it's the lower two chakra's that are hardest to penetrate and need a major breakthrough in order to move up the spine. Ultimately the goal of Shakti is to connect with the rest of the body, Shiva.

The Sanskrit name for this chakra is Swadhisthana, swa meaning "ones own" and adhisthana meaning "dwelling place". It is where a person takes the energy of the First chakra and analyzes its foundation to uncover where some of the root issues lye. Explained more in depth below, its where one's own problems dwell within the body.

The symbolism is a 6-Petaled orange colored lotus that connects us with the element of water and the ebbs and flows of the Moons cycles. It connects us to emotion whether we are conscious of why it has come up or what the emotion is. The Moon in Astrology relates to the way we personalize our lives, our sense of security, and how we soothe ourselves emotionally. The Moon also represents our comfort level and sense of home and family. Its essentially the energy from which we originate. Some women may experience heightened sensitivity and heavens with their periods and both sexes may experience dull or lifeless orgasm and this energy center starts to awaken. While the impulses start to regulate, what once brought us pleasure can now be something we don't care to experience.

This is why so many emotions lay dormant in this area of the body and why it holds many lifetimes of issues that you and your loved one's have been working toward overcoming. The importance of grasping the Moon and its Lunation cycles are of benefit to those who are trying to stimulate and turn on the energies of the Sacral Chakra. Knowing when or looking out for the New Moon and Full Moon is one way to connect to the waxing and waning of the Moon so you are able to observe how you function in between the two week cycle from one to the next. Observing yourself with the Moon is very telling about how you feel at the moment and offers resolve, a smile and a chuckle towards the reality of what life is.

This is the chakra that stores all connections to past life information, traumas and the unconscious. It is here where we compartmentalize our issues for the sake of pressing on. The breath becomes shallow due to low movement of the diaphragm, the prana and apana is cut off at the source and in turn we forget how to breathe through the pain. It is through these past issues and not breathing that we stay blocked and cannot move forward to the Third chakra, the Manipura and the one said to ignite the opening of one's of consciousness. The Location of the Second chakra is the base of the spine, caught between the Root and the Navel. Its also considered the home of the unconscious.

The color of this chakra is orange representing the blending of the lower center (the Root) and the chakra center ahead of it (the Navel)– the red root and yellow navel make an orange Sacral chakra. To help work through the blockages of this energetic center you must utilize what comes up from the foundation of your life and utilize the breath to work through the emotional upheavals.

Being in the Second chakra can look like a person who is doing shadow work. The work of digging deep into the psyche to pull out some semblance of healing grace. When you are activated in this area, you notice that dealing with old patterns in life come up more than you were aware of before. Suddenly problems from childhood, toxic parental relationships, and issues around scarcity make themselves more visible so they can be dealt with. The water element brings with it a sense of creating small tides and over time creating waves, the waves are a collection of small ripples over the course of your life. Each time you feel insecure and go within is linked to a collection of times this has shown itself. You are essentially now dealing with the Root problems and they are ready to be worked out.

Helpful Tool:
5 Crystals/Gems/Stones you can work with by holding, meditating with, visualizing on, or wear as jewelry that assist with the subtle changes in the Sacral Chakra:

Orange Calcite- Helps connect the emotions with intellect and a very active stone by accelerating spiritual growth. Helps to remove negative energies from any space. Helps to alleviate emotional stress and connects you to serenity.

*Topaz-*soothes, heals and stimulates energy in the areas where they are needed most. Helps cut doubt and uncertainty. Inner wisdom is a byproduct as the ques around you confirm what you know and your influence. Great for creative arts.

*Citrine-*activates the Sacral Chakra by stimulating the creative centers of the mind and body. Considered the stone of abundance, it gives you the know how to manifest and attract wealth and prosperity. Enhances concentration and revitalizes the mind. Promotes more joy in life and clears negative and undesirable traits.

Red Jasper- Grounds the energy of the user while rectifying unjust situations. A gentle energy emerges from this stone. Helps provide insight into the most complex situations— clarity can be increased.

Blue Jasper- Helps connect you to the spirit world and balances Yin and Yang energies. Stabilizes the aura and provides sustained energy.

Working with the Sacral Chakra provides a great opportunity to become a part of a community or talk to someone who is specialized in shadow work that can help you understand situations as they arise--To aid in the process of making sense of what happened. Its important to note that these are emotional times and require a great deal of time, attention, verbal processing, and internal digestion. The next step is Journaling what comes up for you— a cathartic process that allows you to spill more about your feelings than you ever could through interaction with another. More about the Journaling process in Chapter 5. The main goal is to "get it out through the communicative process of speech or writing. Holding on to it will only allow the mental process to grow and the possibility of a downward spiral increases.

This chakra makes you alarmingly aware of the material and how you look at and view money, food, love, and sex. When this chakra has been stimulated it starts to look like an abundant life, you are able to buy the things you want so therefore you may have a lot of them. You might look around and wonder where half of these things came from and why you bought them. You then might study your bank account to realize you are very close to spending more than you deposit, another sign you might be going "overboard". Love relationships will start to look bleak as one person after the next shows disappointment rather than hope and successful union. We begin to realize that we extend our bodies to mix and unite with other human beings who have their own energies to work through. Time after time taking in the energy of ever lover until we feel lost and connected to each one emotionally, even after years of separation.

Again, the 2nd chakra is like the first, full of all kinds of things we stow away to be dealt with in the future, however when we deal with them now we feel like the event is happening all over again. While a natural part of life, you now have the opportunity to reshape the way this goes from now on while you work slowly to nurture the parts of you that have been unheard or unfelt for quite some time.

The Third Chakra– Solar Plexus

Sanskrit Name: Manipura Chakra
Associated Color: Yellow
Body Location: The Naval

The third chakra is the place where the action starts to begin, where one starts to control the intensity with how fast they move and progress forward. This chakra controls our projection and breathing process through the diaphragm. It is here the hammer of the navel pounds against the front of the spine to move the lungs and increase breath or "prana" within the body– Yogic Breathing technique called Fire Breath. Buddhist traditions point to this being where the Kundalini Awakens, not the Root chakra. Because it is where consciousness begins to evolve and blossom.

The Sanskrit name for this chakra is Manipura, Mani meaning "jewel" and Pura meaning "city". It is where one takes the energy of the First 2 Chakra's and its foundations to identify where one will start to direct their life in a conscious way. The city of jewels is exactly what it means. When working with the Navel, the breath, prana, we become the driver of the cleansing and clearing of the mind through intentional breathing. The teaching of Prana Apana belongs to this chakra, the devotion of ones life through Yogic breathing takes a breath in Prana(inhale) and expels that breath cleansing and clearing for another, apana (exhale). It is the process of Prana and apana that gets us closer to the path of liberation by fanning the fire of digestion, motivation, the burning away of the past and creating new states of consciousness and a vast array of knowledge that previously wasn't accessible.

Symbolism- the 10-Petaled Lotus and connects with the element of Fire and the natural ebb and flow of the Suns cycles. It connects us to what we actually intend to do with our lives, the proper steps and practices that lead to more energy and opportunity to develop the steps. The Element of Fire burns up what no longer serves, reducing physical or mental matter into ashes– easily able to blow away in the wind. Fire is the ferocity the propels a person to take one more step in a marathon. It can be to cry harder about what moves a person by rapidly moving the belly as deep sobs drive the feeling more intently. It is where the loudness of one's voice resides.

The color of the third chakra is represented by the color Yellow, another visual connection to the Sun, the color gold and the symbolism of power, drive, and strength. This is why it can be known under another pseudonym– The Solar Plexus. The Sun represents our creativity and the ability to derive the self confidence needed to create what needs to be shared with our communities. It's the first sense in realizing what you love is connected to a bigger sense, the individual nature of a person begins to take a more objective approach. Being able to see why we do the things we do and how to make it less about me and more about us. When we take the focus off our own personal attainment, we start working towards the service of others and what your specific gifts offer that make the world go around. Many adjustments are made with this chakra and may be the longest one to get through for some.

The Location of the third chakra is between the naval and the anterior part of the spine. It's the area of our body that contains the kidneys, bladder, digestive tract, metabolism, and is the body temperature control system. It is in this chakra where the heaves of pain can be visually seen and the lungs and belly work together to support you while you release and reach for what will soothe the pain, the heart chakra.

Helpful Tool:

5 Crystals/Gems/Stones you can work with by holding, meditating with, visualizing on, or wear as jewelry that assist with the subtle changes in the Solar Plexus:

Malachite- absorbs negative energies and pollutants such as plutonium and different types of radiation. Activates the chakra's and attunes to the spiritual guidance and vision within a person.

Traditionally known to be the stone of transformation as it encourages risk taking and influences adventure.

Tigers Eye- stimulates the continual rise of the Kundalini. Helps give guidance on correct use of power and clarity of intentions. Helps to balance the hemispheres of the brain. It has the ability to help people who suffer from addictions they would like to change. Tigers eye helps to heal the reproductive organs and aids spiritual grounding when placed directly on the navel.

Yellow Tourmaline- Enhances the personal power of the individual and opens up the pathways and benefits to glean intellectual pursuits and business affairs. For the use of healing it is said to treat the stomach, liver, spleen and Kidneys.

Golden Beryl- teaches you how to do only that which you need to and is excellent is helping aid a stressful life. It is considered a seer's stone and promotes purity of being and walking on this planet. Opens the Crown and Solar Plexus chakra's.

Smithsonite- helps create a buffer against life's problems. Aids in aligning the chakra's and enhancing one's psychic abilities. It has wonderful uses to strengthen the immune system and is said to help against digestive disorders.

Working with the third chakra focuses on what's behind the belly button, it's the core and our strength. One important way to aid in the process of healing this chakra is to clean up the diet and freeing your digestive system from processing so many emotions. More about diet is covered in Chapter 4. Daily breathing practices help realign the metabolism and make the core of the body stronger. Increase in pranayama (Yogic breathing) is what helps Shakti get closer to her goal. It is said that when a person is truly working on themselves the Kundalini will reside in the Naval/Manipura Chakra or higher.

This is the part of the body where it gets strangely clear that you are what you think you are. If you think you are a terrible singer, then well, you will be. If you are determined to be a scholarly leader and author and believe you are before it happens as the gusto to continue moving, you will be that leader and author you wish yourself to be. The Navel is the center that starts to stir the magic of manifestation and breathing through and to the new life you are working to experience.

The Fourth Chakra– The Heart Chakra

Sanskrit Name: Anahata Chakra
Associated Color: Green
Body Location: Behind the sternum/The Heart

The fourth chakra is the place where open hearted compassion lies. Its where we deeply connect with the emotional centers and how we discover in the end– to love them anyways. We never have to think about the heart or tell it when to beat. It opens up and exposes itself to danger for the sake of feeling love and reciprocation from other's. It can also create a shield of protection allowing no one to penetrate the walls, but also keeping you stuck in the lower centers of the body– Shakti wants to unite with Shiva and move up the spine to liberation and happiness.

The Sanskrit name for this chakra is Anahata meaning "un-struck", the continuous beat of the heart does it consistently and in an unbroken rhythm. It's the place in our body that protects our feelings or makes us a beacon for interactions that bring more joy through the expansion of love. Activating this part of the body and continuing to Meditate on its energies will bless the yogic practitioner with elevated capabilities and understanding. Ancient times say this chakra being stimulated turns a yogic practitioner into a full blown yogi, one who knows the posture, the way, the path to love, and one who lives it daily. Like the heart it no longer asks for permission to take another beat, it just does. And so will the yogi who follows the path of the heart and it will lead them deeper into the practices of love and devotion on the divine.

The symbolism is a 12 petaled lotus flower resembling the place where Shiva and Shakti meet. Remember, Shakti is the "serpent" Kundalini that rises up the body once awakened in the hopes to be fully actualized through union and harmonizing energies. This chakra awakens the Air element within the body, clearing the way for joyous disposition, a logical approach and remaining open to refine inner thought processes. Awakening the Air process in the body came from the mastery of the Naval—the prana and apana. Through yogic breathing, meditating on the breath and forcing the emotions up, one sees the light at the end of the tunnel to another center of hope. Digestion of what's occurred to you, the traumas or tensions that reside in your body gets processed through Air and the metronome of the heart. Air is mental capacity and the way we connect to our environments. It is here we look to expand our minds to redefine these events as lessons, to give yourself grace to understand your process and heal.

The color of this chakra is Green as it represents new growth and understanding. Like the Spring flowers that bloom every April, so does the heart as it slowly unfolds revealing the center of its universe. It is a color to remind you of what represents hope and what connects us to the land we reside in, the foods we choose and the lively loving Soul's we find ourselves attracted to. It's the color of being able to move forward and what we look for when selecting particular vegetables to eat. It's the color of abundance and the budding of higher states of consciousness.

The location of this Ccakra encompasses not only the heart, but the lungs as well. As your increased pranayama practices takes off and your lungs start to clear out, get strong and move faster, the heart begins to take on a shape you never knew existed. The feelings that come about are full and complete love for everyone and everything. It then moves to the deepest compassion you've ever had for yourself, you truly see why you have experienced life in the way you have and you are ready to move forward—lessons in hand.

Helpful Tool:
5 Crystals/Gems/Stones you can work with by holding, meditating with, visualizing on, or wear as jewelry that assist with the subtle changes in the Heart chakra:

Rose Quartz- The stone for unconditional love and infinite peace. It reassures the user by helping aid with the healing of trauma's and psychological difficulties. Helps to transmute all heartache and emotions that no longer serve the individual, creating a harmonious state of balance.

Rhodonite- This stone is an emotional balancer restoring faith and nurtures love and encourages the brotherhood of humanity. Helps to clear away emotional wounds of the past. Assisting in the forgiveness needed to reconcile after long-term abuse and pain. This stone has the ability to heal abandonment and betrayal.

Watermelon Tourmaline- the "super activator" of the heart chakra. It helps instill patience, tact and diplomacy. Assists in dissolving any resistance to becoming whole and befits the dynamic of your relationships and helps you find the joy in situations.

Peridot- Releases old baggage and burdens of guilt and obsessiveness. A powerful cleanser and activator of the Heart and Solar Plexus chakra's. A gem that teaches that holding on to people and material possessions and ideation's of the past are counterproductive. It aids in helping you to look to your own higher energies for guidance.

Amazonite- The stone has an extremely soothing property calming the brain and the nervous system. It balances the masculine and feminine energies and restores health in many damaged relationship dynamics. Helps to alleviate worry and fear.

The process of healing the heart chakra is a long and arduous task for those that have thick inner walls around their connection to people, trauma, and trust. Listening to music is one way to connect because the sequence of notes tie you to bigger parts of the natural world. Keep your heart open during music sessions. Mantra Yoga offers another perspective to life as singing the word of God and opening to devotion can amplify your Heart chakra for all to see, and hear.

Another beneficial and safe way to tap into the powerful force behind the heart chakra is to be in nature, connecting to all to all of the color green you can, again, the idea is to remove yourself from your personal environment and to experience the vastness around you. Take in scenery that makes your heart swell with joy and happiness. If this is not accessible for you, it is recommended you connect to the scenery you do have access to whether it be digital, photographs or video chats with friends in places that can help you connect. You are never limited by your circumstance, location, race, gender, identification, or sexual orientation. We utilize the tools we have in the spaces we were given to work with and prove once again that the Kundalini lives and moves inside of each and every one of us, no matter what kind of life we were born into.

Being in the heart and having this activation brings about a lot situations and feel like they need to be forgiven or that you need to increase your compassion for the people involved instead of holding tight to your previous beliefs. You may find yourself reaching out to people you haven't spoken to in ages, willing to rebuild bridges of friendship and finally putting to bed all the expectation that led to disappointment.

Being in the heart chakra also looks like something different to other people. You become a beacon of health and radiation because that is what love inhabits. Your chest will be up, out, and proud and you elongate your neck for the open activation of the throat chakra when it is time. People will start to come to you for help at this point because you will begin to take on the look of someone who knows a few things and has been around the block to know. The hard work will stop looking like something crazy to other people because the change within you has become a positive step for all, not just a personal self journey that includes no one. Your inclusion, openness, and drive to allow things to fall that no longer provide value will be insurmountable. Giving when you have extra can be soothing to this stage and a bright open smile is the one free thing you can give aplenty to anyone you feel safe with.

You will come to realize that holding on to anything emotionally doesn't serve the highest good of who you are. Saying sorry, saying goodbye, and smiling a little more are common themes. Some days you'll look around and wonder what you did to deserve this little moment of pure joy and you can always thank the heavens and your determination that hold you here, in the space where you start to come alive and move into the process of speaking your new truth which begins to occur in the 5th chakra.

The Fifth Chakra— The Throat Chakra

Sanskrit Name: Vishuddhi Chakra
Associated Color: Blue
Body Location: The Throat

The fifth chakra is where truth comes and its less about what you say and more about what you hear and sense. The Throat chakra is the place where voice is established and what is projected to others. When you know your truth, there isn't much to say about it, you feel no particular reason to shout it out to anyone and you care less about being right and care more about being open to the possibility of anything happening. Adventure and wonderment returns here.

The Sanskrit name is the Vishuddhi chakra, shuddhi meaning to purify, this chakra stands for purification. It is through purification one can ensure the longevity of their life and that is through careful consumption and accepting who you are in life by what you can change and what you cannot. Purification lends itself to words, what are you no longer willing to say out loud because its no longer true for you? Who are you no longer willing to talk about because it doesn't make you feel good? What will you make vocal to others about what you will tolerate and what you can no longer put up with?

The color of this chakra is Blue representing the vast open sky's that cover all of the world and the depths of oceans and seas below it. What remains in the middle of these vast bodies is a reality that is removed from ego and more connected to the wholeness. This lotus with 16-petals gives a person the power to move with conviction and ease as parts of a person settle, anger becomes a chuckle, sadness becomes contemplation, and heaviness turns into a time of self care. This is what it means to understand who you are and what you can and cannot change about yourself–it softens the spirit and increases vocabulary.

The location is right behind the throat or voice box and would encompass everything around the jaw line, the neck and shoulders. Working with this energy can bring a massive change in habits as you let go of the last ones you are no longer connected or feel you need. This becomes like stated above, a purification process of what is taken in as "food". Not all sustenance is in the form of something you take in through the mouth, it does include what you allow others to say to you and what you are able to pick up on you environment. Empathetic reactions towards your environment may become more intense as you start to feel the energy of others more. This further adds to the understanding and compassion that was activated with the Heart chakra.

Helpful Tool:
5 Crystals/Gems/Stones you can work with by holding, meditating with, visualizing on, or wear as jewelry that assist with the subtle changes in the throat chakra:

Azurite- Guides in psychic and intuitive development and urges the soul to seek enlightenment. Safe journeys in and out of the body can be used with this stone. Mentally brings about clear understanding and expands the mind. Has the ability to reshape belief systems and search for the deeper truths.

Turquoise- promotes spiritual attunement and enhances communication with the physical and spiritual worlds. A promoter of self-realization, assists in creative problem solving and creative expression. It is a stone that strengthens the fortitude of a person and works well for panic attacks, anxiety, exhaustion, and depression.

Amethyst- boost the production of hormones and attunes the endocrine system and metabolism. Enhances higher states of concentration and Meditation. Promotes love of the divine, encourages selflessness and spiritual wisdom. Improves motivation and keeps you from setting unrealistic goals.

Amber- A fossilized tree resin that has strong connections to the Earth and other higher energies. Helps link the everyday self to the spiritual life. Promotes a positive mental state and helps clear away negative connotations, pain and beliefs. Helps to treat and clear throat problems.

Kunzite- Helps induce a deep meditative state and is a highly spiritual stone. This stone is best to use if a person is having a hard time getting into the meditative state. Helps protect the aura from unwanted energies. Facilitates introspection and the ability to act on constructive criticism.

There are many things you can do to support the throat chakra as it slowly begins to open up and experience how it wants to participate in the world. First, lets acknowledge that reaching this step is no easy feat and the things you have come across in your journey makes you a person of varied experience. A congratulations to you if you notice and connect to the words in this part of the book. It means you have either activated the Throat already or are awakening to the process. Take a moment to take full stock of where you have been.

The things you hear, taste, touch, smell and talk about will all suddenly change and the people around you will not only take notice, but start to inquire about how to get what it is you have. Waiting until you are asked not only instills your authority because you look like a person who knows, but you savor the moments of explaining what it is you know—finally! People will be mesmerized because the tone of your voice and the development of the throat begins to mature like that of a wisdom keeper.

The throat chakra gives a person room to use their voice, usually when someone has this area activated and has a problem standing up for themselves all the sudden feel embolden to say no, or to offer an opinion that goes against the group narrative. Autonomy and a sure sense of sovereignty. Suddenly it will feel okay to be who you are out loud.

The Six Chakra— The Third Eye

Sanskrit Name: Ajna Chakra
Associated Color: Indigo
Body Location: Between the Eyebrows

The Sixth chakra is the place that projects between the middle of the brow, the place that furrows when you don't understand something from a mental stance. However its actual location resides at the tip of the spine and can be said to represent the Eye of Shiva. It is located in the area of our head where sight beyond sight occurs.

The Sanskrit name is the Ajna chakra, Ajna meaning "to know, to obey or to follow" and is faithfully known as the "Guru chakra" because of its intuition enhancing abilities. What's meant by this is an understanding that there is a higher power at work to help guide you to happiness. You obey or follow the directions of the inner self to get to higher planes of thinking and better ways of living a quality life. Devotion to a higher purpose, power, or service comes with this stimulation. It creates all kinds of intuitive knowing's that offer more chances to take "safe" risks.

When there is a goal to life and a focus on the picture outside of self gratification, opportunities to be of service, materials needed to start the project begin to surface, and the people needed to network help you connect the missing links. It leads you to people like yourself who have similar goals, while some of these groups will be small, the impact is what matters most. The value of this chakra is pertinent to self improvement and knowing oneself fully. When you are focused and centered within you care less about what others are doing and more about how you will get to the higher points of life, the more you will try to experience for yourself and the more you begin to make yourself an autonomous entity– enjoying time alone and contemplating /manifesting the life you wish to continue.

The symbolism of this chakra is a 2 petaled lotus with a circle in the middle and is a physical representation of the eyes. However this eye in the middle is not exactly opened outward, instead its closed focusing on the being within–staring at the Soul to see what it needs next. Meditation is the one true practice that has us close all eyes to give the Third Eye more attention. Its what we see behind the eyelids and what we find staring back at us is not only a superb display of magic, but also holds the ability to bring to life visions of past, present and future memory.

It can really show itself as innumerable possibilities, the idea is to allow the process to unfold for yourself without expectation. Having these kinds of sights will not feel scary or overwhelming if you are ready and actually activated to take it on. Slow down if you feel as if this process increases ideation's that may not seem like yours. You ultimately want the decisions you make and the thoughts you think to be your own and in a space to receive that feels comfortable and safe to navigate. Listening to yourself is an important feature during this opening and nurturing of the Third Eye chakra.

The color of this chakra is Indigo a represents a color that is not commonly seen, but is recognized as magnificence when it is seen. It is a color of blue that offers a vibrancy and state of well-being and that is a close comparison to the chakra itself, as many who try to attain this awakening loose sight and need reminders, this color will offer that. There are the desert people of Tuareg people who shine brightly in the Sun with Indigo materials draped over their bodies. Bright, happy, devoted people who take the situation they are presented and not only thrive while doing it, but make it absolutely beautiful. It's a color that represents Royal or Imperial bloodline and is one of the true colors of staying connected to your ancestral roots– feeling and seeing the intuitive practices, preparing elixirs, spontaneous body movements, and ceremonies you have internal access to, but maybe were not trained in.

The location actually isn't on the outside of the skin or in the front of the head per se, the projection is made between the eye brows slightly above the eye sockets, but again is located at the back of the skull. This area on the outside is a point of tension for many as they try to guide their way carefully through life's obstacles in a mental sense. After all, this is the chakra of the mind and higher mental capacities. It's a higher sight than the eyes and sits exactly where the spinal cord ends. When Shakti has made her way up through the spine to bring a person to complete bliss, she is reminded she will meet yet again with Shiva as he offers the blessing of a sight beyond sight. Your journey is believed to be protected and guided forward to the next level of liberation, the 7th chakra.

Helpful Tool:
5 Crystals/Gems/Stones you can work with by holding, meditating with, visualizing on, or wear as jewelry that assist with the subtle changes in the Third Eye:

Sodalite- helps to unite logic by using your intuition, also aids in expanding spiritual perceptions and bringing the higher mind into the physical realm. This stone can be used to understand the circumstances you find yourself in. It stimulates trust and companionship between members of a group, encouraging interdependence. Helps release core fears, phobias, biases and guilt.

Diamond- clears emotional and mental pain, reducing fear while bringing about new beginnings.

Helps to pinpoint anything that is negative and requires transformation. The inner light and soul shines through a person that wears a diamond. It not only works as a creative stone but helps stimulate the imagination and inventiveness of your new projects.

Lapis Lazuli- is said to open the Third Eye and helps to balance the throat chakra. Stimulates the chances for enlightenment and aids someone in working with their dream state. Helps to bring in deep inner self-knowledge. Works as a powerful thought amplifier by stimulating the higher faculties of the mind. Encourages taking charge of one's life.

Garnet- cleanses and re-energizes the body and the chakra system. Inspires love and devotion, perfect for Mantra Yoga. It can stimulate past life memory and aid in past life regression work. Activates and amplifies other stones in its proximity.

Purple Fluorite- assists in imparting common sense to psychic communication. Great to use for Meditation. High level psychic protection and heightens intuitive powers and liking to the Universal mind.

Taking care to allow this chakra to blossom as it needs to involves rigorous practice and dedication. Mantra Yoga is one of the best remedies to keep this eye focused within, that is what concentrating on spiritual words does, it asks for the blessings of the particular God, deity, manifestation, or loving words and uses it to quiet the mind so intuitive messages can be heard. Mediation is another way to nurture the quieting of the mind and gives you the positive reinforcement that its okay to be where you are in the moment. Any practice that gets you closer to looking at the self will be of benefit and researching specific parts of yourself may feel like the next step. Your ancestry may become of more importance, your interest in studying the occult or medicinal practices may unfold as an unlikely attraction, hobby, or adopted way of life.

With the stimulation of the Third Eye chakra the sense and purposeful drive of individuality lessons and with time becomes more wholly centered around the concept of interdependence. It's the idea that you can always be yourself and contribute your unique gifts to the collective of the group. It then becomes a mass of people such as yourself offering to the world what they consider to be valuable, how they get to higher states of wealth by working independently together as a fully functioning unit. When other people emit this frequency, you quickly realize they are a part of your group, tribe, soul family, or whatever you call people you feel you've known for a long time, but in actuality, haven't. The focus should be to polish your skills and become a master of your domain, whatever that is. When you do this, you become a beacon for people who need your services and the chance to match up with similar frequencies such as yourself.

The Seventh Chakra– The Crown Chakra

Sanskrit Name: Sahasrara Chakra
Associated Color: Violet/Purple
Body Location: The Top of the Head

The seventh chakra is the place where Shiva and Shakti finally meet at the top of the head. It is the complete and total Awakening of the Kundalini and all its faculties. From the Root chakra to the Third Eye, everything is pushed past just an activation or stimulation of the chakra's.

The Sanskrit name is the Sahasrara shakra the "one thousand" an is to represent the nadis (energetic loops) that wrap around the entire body and helping the central wiring system (nervous system) stay alert and on command as a high intelligence that helps you navigate the world and to feel comfortable while doing it.

The symbolism of this chakra is the Thousand petaled lotus, again representing the central system of all functions.

The color of this chakra is Violet, representing the periodical colors of spring and summer that show an individual what it means to be alive. This color can be seen behind the eyes when in deep meditative states. This color is the sign of enlightenment and union with the self. It is the fullness of understanding and the practice of the Kundalini– self-study. This color can be worn or furnished to remind you of the vastness outside of your experience and the pure energy that emanates from you because of you diligent Yogic practice and focus toward the inward journey of self knowledge.

The location of this chakra is on the top of the head, over the soft spot of a newborn skull. It is a physical representation of as above, so below. What happens out there, happens in here. It's the connection between the physical body and the portal to the ethereal. What happens for a person beyond this measure is said to be of 7 higher spiritual centers that connect a person more with heaven, God, the Universe, The All, it's a recognition that there is something out there, beyond you, your thinking, your experiences, and your sight. With that said, the varying degrees of what can happen for and to a person can only become clear as more people experience the phenomena of Awakening there own Kundalini– a natural born right to those on the path.

Helpful Tool:
5 Crystals/Gems/Stones you can work with by holding, meditating with, visualizing on, or wear as jewelry that assist with the subtle changes with the Crown chakra.

Red Serpentine- a grounding stone that aids in Meditation and spiritual contemplation. Helps to make you feel more in control of your life. Helps to ensure longevity by promoting purification and cleansing. Works to correct emotional imbalances and gaps in consciousness.

Purple Jasper- eliminates contradictions and activates the Crown chakra. Facilitates Shamanic journeys and dream recollection. Aids in quick thinking and promotes organizational abilities. Encourages honesty within yourself and aids in heightening intuitive abilities and sense of direction. Helps align the chakra's.

Moldavite- it is said to have extraterrestrial origin, formed when a giant meteorite struck the earth. It is a fusion of crystals over a vast area. Helps take other crystals to their highest vibration. Can aid in putting you in touch with Ascended Masters and cosmic messengers of the past. Helps to accelerate spiritual growth. This stone is said to create properties that can send a person over the edge, use with caution and ask your supplier about the best ways to keep its energy stable.

Citrine- activates the Crown chakra by opening up the intuition. Considered the stone of abundance, it gives you the know how to manifest and attract wealth and prosperity. Enhances concentration and revitalizes the mind. Promotes more joy in life and clears negative and undesirable traits.

Lepidolite- clears blockages and brings cosmic awareness. Tunes you into thoughts and feelings from other lives. Enhances standing in your own space and free from the influence of others. Helps to release mental and emotional dependancy on others and ridding oneself from the common complaints of life.

To gain the knowledge and steps needed to nurture this chakra, it is important to note that the other chakra's need the time and attention to help keep the body attuned to higher frequencies. The previous Six Chakra's are like light switches, turning on with each indication that you are ready to move on, getting you closer to the end goal of awakening. All of the chakra's serve as area's of reference to continually check in and participate with. The practices outlined in SECTION 3: THE PRACTICE AND THE JOURNEY will offer you the beginning steps to understanding yourself at a deeper level.

The full purpose of the Crown chakra is to bring back the reminder that nothing is outside of yourself. Your wealth comes from the inside though what you value and the resources you're able to manifest, not the actual material itself. The internal motivation it takes to lead yourself down a road of resourcefulness comes from the personal need to make it so. If nothing is outside of yourself than love is not something you need from others, its enough for you to give love to yourself, love is inside of you. You are not more lovable because someone else says you are. Happiness can be fleeting, some people make happiness centered around the circumstance turning out well instead of a consistent form of happiness that is not reliant on any particular event, place, or person—its something you choose to wake up with. When you have reached this center and are working with the activation of this chakra, happiness comes effortlessly and the spread of this feeling is contagious. The Crown chakra is the connection to a vast system of knowledge, intuition, and spiritual understanding. It is the area that connects us to the higher realms of heaven

CHAPTER FOUR
Creating Space For The Practices of Awakening

The best ways to absorb the fresh energies you are awakening to, its important to note how environment plays such a large roll in how we take in and process information. When you are able to curate a clean, minimal and intentional space, the world opens up and the mind begins to unwind. There are quite a few things we can do to tidy up our spaces to not be a show of perfection, but rather an example of your mental state. Sometimes the state of a persons home is a reflection of their mind state. If you find your things strewn around your space, not having a home for any particular item and still have boxes from moving 5 months ago collecting dust in the corner, then you might have a scattered mind space. Some people feel physical comfort having a home filled and placing things where they lay. You notice they still function to a mildly effective degree, but always scurrying to clean a spot for you to sit or apologizing for the cleaning they never intend to do.

Say your house is filled with beautiful art, tapestries, pictures of trips, and brightly colored accents, and this brings you full and complete joy– keep this. If you feel there are some things you'd like to change and there would be a way to beautify your space– do this. The idea is to always nurture and curate a space that when you look at it from across the room or stumble into it first thing in the morning to start you day, you are proud, feel positive and are ready to spend time in that space. Happiness is the name of the game and you ultimately want all of your spaces to inspire this emotion and feeling within you.

A sense of pride over your home can be established, no matter where that is. Whether you travel full time encompassing many different types of spaces or you travel on the road in your own private space, you are brought to resonance when the things you love, the things that create value in your life are present. That can mean your favorite pair of shoes, a prayer altar, or fresh clean linens. For those of us who don't move around the world and change our surroundings often, refreshing, de-cluttering, and keeping the corners of your house clean are simple yet effective ways to attain a sense of physical peace and organization of the material– allowing the ethereal to come into view with ease.

Consider some of the most beautiful and comfortable surroundings you've been in to date, what's the common theme among them, if any? Can these feelings of comfort be recreated in real time?

The colors, patterns, drapery, that fluffy pillow or amazing shag rug, what are the physical things that connect you deeply to color, imagination, or creativity? What can you create in your home that has a resemblance of nature and the 5-senses? Are you a plant lover with a green thumb or need to have a fish tank because the running water soothes you? Do you have the scents in candle, oil, or incense form that soothe your sense of smell? One way to compartmentalize all of your stuff is to give it a purpose assigned to these requirements, what you need and the consistency of your emotional and environmental well-being.

Getting rid of things is one way to purge, it's a physical representation of letting go and moving on. Just remember that the things you own could be of value to the less fortunate. Why donating is a wonderful way to get started, your items could be better served for programs that serve under represented people, giving them access to these items for free instead of walking into a donation center to pay a lesser price. Be sure to take the extra time to find these places so you can connect deeper to the process of letting go, knowing the faces and reasons why people will now use the items you are graciously giving away. This process can really feel good for everyone if you involve yourself in the process a little more– whatever you do, remember that it is enough.

The practice of creating a space that's conducive to a good life and supportive of our practices is a large step in the process of your mental evolution—again, a physical representation of what you feel like on the inside. Not perfection, but carefully though about and put together. Shifting the world around you so that you're able to see the change as you await the feelings of it is a great way to accelerate the process of Awakening to your higher senses. You then become a magician of your environment, creating processes and spaces that intuitively connect to your emotional process and quiet delicate practices of going within.

Your Sleeping Practice

The place you lay your head at night is the most important place on the planet. Sleep is pertinent to the human life function and when something is off in this space it sends a chain of reactions to occur that make you wonder what to do to fix the situation. Many people have been fatigued for so long they have no idea the reason they aren't feeling well is because they regularity don't get enough rest. What this turns into is an over consumption of products, powders, blended drinks, coffee, mineral infused mud and so much more. These products, while amazing and innovative in their creation, help highlight an important issue in the way we move through our lives and how we feel from day to day– we need something else to feel good.

According to the Sleep Foundation, sleep apnea, a condition where a person will stop breathing for sections of time impairing there ability to get a restful nights sleep because oxygen airways are physically obstructed. If you feel you suffer from this condition its best to speak with your medical doctor about the options you have for treatment. Above all the number of people getting tested for this condition is skyrocketing and as you have learned above, when you cannot breathe properly, when the prana and apana are held back in any way the quality of life is severely diminished. Symptoms of sleep depravation look closely like having a terrible day. Headaches, snoring, extreme dry mouth, irritability, mid-day sleepiness, reliance on stimulants, trouble breathing, and many other reactions point to a bigger picture of not being able to fully enjoy the life you were meant to have. Sleep is one of the number one things we need to do well.

The amount of sleep we get isn't as important as the quality is, and the quality is what's measured. You can spend a good 8 to 10 hours rolling around in the bed tossing the blankets and shuffling the pillows, remembering every random thought that passed through your brain while angrily sipping coffee. Or you can get a nice 6 to 8 hours of restful sleep where you don't remember moving around, using the bathroom, or anything else but the dream that still has you mesmerized, or freaked out. As you work through the Kundalini and utilize your Yogic tools of practice, you may come to realize that the quality of sleep increases while the amount of sleep you need decreases. 5 to 6 hours feels right to a person with rigorous practice and a purposeful life to wake up to.

You may be thinking of ways to improve your sleep by buying the latest pillow or roll up mattress shipped to your door, but the importance is to understand the physiology of the body and support it during its natural process instead of going against it. Now and days we are marketed to as if we have no connection to what our experience is, in fact in some cases we are told how we feel, given quirky and memorable examples and by the end you are ready to give your credit card information. Be careful of falling prey to buying the next new thing that is touted as the cure all to better posture, sleep, focus or capabilities. Decide for yourself what you are looking for in a product and then go find the item yourself, try your best to avoid advertisements and marketing strategies that are linked to your search history or phone. You don't need to be followed and then sold to, you are an open minded and self-knowledge directed and your purchases should reflect your conscious buying.

Pillows, do we need them? Through time the way we sleep has been depicted in many different ways, minimal items were used in civilizations that were considered highly intelligent like the Egyptians and as time evolved the number of items and cotton filled things strewn the across the bed has grown exponentially. The ideal look of a plush bed and headboard can make any sleep enthusiast scream for joy and jump in, but what happens to that body when it is 36, not so limber, and has a meeting at 6am? Pillows, while seemingly supportive of the head does nothing more than create obstruction to the airways for many. Back sleepers are recommended to use a small roll under the neck or a flat pillow rolled to support the back of the head. This not only allows the body to fully lay straight, but the airway is completely aligned as the throat remains open for proper inhale and exhalation. Side sleepers are encouraged to utilize pillows for the support of pressure points. One medium pillow under the head, one between the legs to stabilize the hips and one in front of the body to support your free arm. While it may seem like a lot, you are giving your body the alignment it needs to support your sleeping arrangement. Stomach sleepers are encouraged to sleep with no pillow as it creates a large s-shape in the back as the upper body is disproportionately higher than the lower half.

Mattresses and blankets are up for your discretion, but the common goal for these is to have a blanket that matches the needs of a room that is below 70 degrees Fahrenheit (60-67 is ideal) and a firm mattress that supports the body. Some people sleep closer to the ground on a mat or literally the ground itself and they feel supported and sleep well as the body adapts to the ancestral ways we used to sleep, before plush beds with frames. Many Yogis recommend sleeping on the floor or under a thin mat for the best sleep. Initially the body will be sore as it tries to adapt, but over time you will realize how strong your body feels and how effortless it feels to get out of bed. The temperature of the place you sleep is of great importance because between the range of 60-65F or 15-20C the body starts to produce the hormone Melatonin for sleep. This temperature also increases the chance you will go into REM sleep which is the deepest sleep a person experiences to feel restful.

Cleanliness of space and items in the room. For the best sleep, it is better to have free and clear energy of the space if possible. Some people sleep in a Van or RV, and some live in a studio with no separate space to sleep, so use your best judgment when adjusting any of the items of your space— it doesn't need to be perfect. The corners of the room should always be cleaned out as they can store unwanted energies and emotions, allowing them to stay in your space for long periods of time. Clutter near your head or a cell phone can greatly reduce the quality of sleep due to EMF (electromagnetic fog) and the energy stored in those items. If you need an alarm clock, you should get one, it should no longer be your phone– if you can help it. People who work on-call or are responsible for someone else should do what's best for their situation.

For sleeping in alignment with the hemispheres of the earth and the Sun's travel across the ecliptic, sleep with your head facing East as the Sun rises and the feet facing West as the Sun sets. This is an ancient and old Yogic practice of positioning yourself so that you create as much balance as humanly possible.

When you consider all the factors that go into sleep you realize there are so many connections to make when you are trying to bring it to a state of quality and when you are not connected, it results in the form of chaos. Remember, chaos is only a sign that things are getting ready to change and adapt to something new, no need to feel guilty about the way life presents itself and the way we react, all we can do is make the small steps needed to gently redirect our experience of chaos and recognize it as a sign that more attention needs to be given to one aspect of life.

Its important to note that not everyone needs to change the way they sleep, some people are perfectly content on the amount, quality and style they practice to get the best benefit. In no way are we directing what your experience should be, its only suggestions for those who feel their situation could or should be improved. Sleep is important overall function and well-being of life is something everyone needs to feel optimal, you deserve to sleep and to sleep well.

Your Kitchen: Treating Food as Medicine

Believe it or not, spirituality does include more than the actual practices to get there. As stated before, its an all encompassing transformation that occurs with diligence and discipline towards new routines that are fit for your body, mind, and Soul. Here we will not discuss diet, but more so speak on the energy of certain types of foods and when to use them for your beneficial gain—nothing in excess if at all possible. What you will come to realize during the Naval chakra work, is that the belly is not aligned with the mental faculties, after all, some scientists and studies say our second brain in is the gut. In this section, we intend to cover areas of food that empower you to make informed decisions and to take away the guilt of wanting or needing a particular food to be used as medicine. Food as medicine is an old age adage about consuming that which heals and protects you on your journey by staying away from the things that deter you and aid in the degeneration in your nutrient levels and pocket books.

People say that in order to achieve this, you must be organic, vegan, vegetarian, or have access to alternative milks, packaged delivery meals, and an endless amount of powders and potions that tout food on the label. This simply isn't true, you don't need to have access to anything fancy, what you do need access to is whole foods. Whole beans, rice, meats, cheeses, flour to make pastas and breads, whole eggs, milk you love, and fruits/vegetables that are fresh, dehydrated or had been flash frozen for freshness. You pay more for boxes and bags of foods found in the isles that are pre made then you would if you took 1 day out of your week to prepare 2 of the foods on your list from the freshest ingredients you could—possibly holding left overs to freeze for another day. If you have the means for any of the options where you purify your diet by eliminating food groups and replacing them with healthier options, you should, however take care to what you eliminate and supplementation may be necessary to fill in the gaps. Say you give up red meat, you will need to find a good iron and fat source to fill the place. While the body takes a lot of time to process a steak there are many benefits phsically, like being able to consume its nutrients, getting healthy skin, nails and hair through collagen and vitamins we cannot produce without consumption of meat like B-12.

It is with sincerity you have the opportunity to try out different ways of eating by eliminating foods that no longer serve your mobility, nervous system, or brain function. What fuels your body does not fuel the next body in the same way so honestly listening to yourself by analyzing the way the food makes you feel is where the journey begins. Awakening the Kundalini and opening the Third Eye makes you conscious about your food choices and makes you get creative on ways to seek out what you need and finding the means to change an unhealthy situation. Don't worry, not all of this comes at once, but you will begin to see it in your awareness, and in all actuality, food is what may have brought you here. More below on the magic of food.

Tapping Into The Senses

The idea is to absorb as much as you can mentally, but moving forward, take notice of how you feel after certain meals, being out with particular people or noticing when the vibe is off. There is an intuitive and instinctual connection to our foods, we are enticed by color, texture, ambiance and location as well as knowing what foods we desire to consume that "feed" us. Not only do we really want to just scarf down a burger because we haven't eaten all day, but in actuality we want to feel as if love was put in it, where you take an bite and say out loud "wow", and maybe slow down to savor the flavor, juices, crispness of the lettuce or the softly toasted bun. Notice your senses liven as these parts of the Kundalini being stimulated, this part can be fun as you rediscover what nourishes and feeds you internally with love. Focusing on the taste and smell senses can make food feel more enjoyable and can ultimately feel more satisfying.

Using Intuition-Let Food Choose You

One of the most enjoyable experiences is eating foods you were so happy you chose because now, you feel satiated—a need has been met. However its much deeper as you look around and realize why you eat the foods you do, shop at the places you do for food, and where you consume food outside of your home. In a rapidly moving era, we have completely changed the way we consume food. People now eat it cold as they pull out their phone and start ordering from their favorite spot, they have eaten their personally so many times that now they order in. The box, bag, or contraption that is trapped to the back of a biker or in someone's car in traffic is increasing in appeal to many. The ease of ordering what you want without thinking too much on if you have the ingredients to make it yourself, or change out of your clothes to look presentable to go pick it up or dine in is convenient. However, what exactly, is so convenient about reheating your food in the microwave or oven, not knowing who exactly touched it, who took your order, or had a good energy to eat at?

When we choose a place to walk in while taking a stroll or going in with a friend to try something new, we always get more intuitive ques on what to choose. It could be the name, location of the place, your favorite flowers on the table, or just all around amazing reviews and photos of the food. You go based on what you have a taste for, combined with where to soothe that energy and the best frequency possible. When you arrive to order you hope the staff is friendly and attentive, that people like where they work– when you like your work, you do good work and that can be seen in any establishment by the employee moral and happiness you witness. You get a table and quicky realize your waiter has the same name as your favorite person, they chat you up and give you recommendations about what to eat next and where to go to make your journey more complete. This must be done with an open heart and a willingness to connect to people who are in service to your needs or improve or simplify your life in any way. This approach makes you smile with joy because it has exceeded your expectation in a very physical way. It goes far beyond the food and much more about connecting to people outside of yourself by asking how their day is and giving them the support they need if they are willing to accept it— the energy exchange can be extremely high and invigorating when experienced on a consistent basis.

Lets talk about intuitive eating at home, what do you have in your kitchen that sounds good right now? What usually sounds good mimics the opportunities of going out to get food, only the flavors, ingredients and timing are all within your control. When we crave certain foods there is a nutrient, mineral, or vitamin that the body usually is asking for and it remembers very viscerally what foods it should consume to get the most of this nutrient the body desires.

Do you have fresh ingredients like fresh vegetables and fruit, or maybe you have the frozen versions which are just as amazing and gives you creativity. Are you in a good mood, or do you feel like cooking? These are all factors to consider a few hours before you consume a meal so your planning, motivation and creativity to invent or recreate a recipe becomes easier to slip into. If you aren't a person who normally cooks or eats at home in this way, you can start with meals that are easy to prepare and begin with 1 to 2 days a week to see how you feel. Not everyone cooks, but everyone needs to eat and brining food home is a great way to fill yourself with the nourishment. Whether it be a bunch of bananas, an apple that called to you, or a nice loaf of bread, those simple things can make all the difference in whether we can feel lack or feel full of life.

Letting food choose you is taking a step back and taking a few more moments in the day to contemplate about how you will fuel your body. Picking the freshest and best quality ingredients you can find of the foods you want to eat propels your success and opportunity of flavor and all around enjoyment. Letting foods choose you can also look like taking stock of what you have in your cupboards, pantries and counter tops, scanning what you have to see what visually jumps out at you. You tend to find foods you didn't know you had and that are still fresh to consume, adding to the joy and grateful feelings of having done a small gesture of taking in food visually and allowing it to come to you.

When Food Opens You Up

When you clean up your diet, over time you start to sense more about your surroundings, the types of places you will eat at and how often you cook at home. It will become more important to you to gain control over ingredients, quality and time. With this, conscious eating begins and you ultimately fine tune your intuitive food selection and know when to allow them to choose you.

Vegans experience a lightness that most other ways of eating don't achieve, unless the person is heavily reliant on processed cheeses and fake meats, then the diet is the same if not worse than a diet filled with no real nutrition. The removal of dairy allows the body to tame its histamine receptors and inflammation can be decreased exponentially. As breads are harder to consume, a person may stay away from refined carbohydrates by proxy so long as the replacements are not over consumption of other carbohydrate heavy foods that take the body a long time to break down and create excesses of sugars and waste lines.

While Vegetarians get a few more freedoms in terms of foods, they still have the same issues as Vegans will run into, not enough fat sources easily available, heavy reliance on carbohydrates when mentally low or unmotivated. The experience can be an increased want or need to insert variety by consuming packaged meatless substitutes and meals out on the market.

The Standard Diet of any country you live in has morphed into something different since the ending of the Second World War. Packaged convenience foods have been a staple of these diets, most are heavy in meat portions or contain too many fats or sugars that render the body slower and less equipped to obtain the body type or health that's needed. These foods that are "standard" in nature usually practice conventional farming and manufacturing processes that completely remove the consumer from the food they consume and where it comes from. This happens all over the world, no one is exempt from falling into the pits of unhealthy eating and not knowing how to transform it. While the higher people on the rung decide what is mainstream to eat, you will need to take back those decisions by diversifying your options if at all possible. If you live in a space with a patio or backyard, consider growing 1 or 2 things you love and see how the what can eat open up your heart, mind and overall experience.

While we only name a few type of diets here, there are hundreds more that have touted the latest trends in nutrient management and reduction of foods to increase overall senses of well being. Its really up to you to do the research when it comes upon you, when you have been thinking about making a change for a while, but are curious to know what your options are. These diets were also mentioned because it is a spectrum of eating styles you will find in a common Yoga class or people who find themselves on the spiritual path. When we talk of Yogis, we talk of purification, and the reduction of animal products and energies, so that spiritual intensity increases—less inhibited by what is consumed. When your options and decisions contain diversity and openness of mind, food can truly open you up to let you know where you are on your journey.

What you put in your body is just as valuable as what you don't put in your body and in terms of fasting, you might consider this a part of your regimen to stay healthy. Fasting is not for everyone, so please consult your doctor before taking on a rigorous restrictions such as abstaining from solids and only consuming fluids. Fasting can be considered a daily practice and is as simple as spreading out your meals so that the bulk of you not eating is when you are resting. For example, if you stop eating 3 to 4 hours before you go to bed, you will give your body time to process and slow down before you rest. You'll now add your sleep which should healthfully be between 6 and 8 hours each night. You'll then add the hours after you wake before you break your fast. If your sum total adds up to more than 11 hours of not eating, you are on the right track to supreme digestion, a daily practice of limiting intake past physical exertion, and a sense of internal wellness within days of implementation.

How You Store Your Food Matters

How you store your food and where you put it is an important factor when considering the energy of your food and amplifying its medicinal qualities by having it in places that can be seen, areas that are clean, and keeping up with expiration. Keeping your refrigerator free and clear of old foods or too many foods for that matter will greatly increase the chances of you finishing all of the food you bough for the fridge. Waste occurs a lot often when things are shoved in drawers below things that last a long time, in turn because it is underneath and unseen, it spoils. It forces you to waste, even minuscule amounts of food that make you exclaim out loud, "ah man", I wanted to eat that.

How often do you leave left overs in your fridge from places you've eaten out? Limit their life in your life to one day after original consumption. If you did not prepare the food yourself, you can expect the shelf life to be extremely narrow. How many condiments are on the door of your fridge that you don't really use, like, or have an expiration date that is overdue? Cleaning these out helps increase your chances of success. When they are not present to cloud your judgment or force you to autopilot scan, you are more focused on what's fresh and in front of your face.

When you bring food home from the grocery store, how do you put it away and keep it stored? Is it trapped in the plastic bag you put it in before placing it in your cart, or do you carefully wash, cut and place in a container for lasting freshness? You are encouraged to get these bags off your vegetables so they can breathe. Storing lettuce freshly cleaned, washed and wrapped in wet paper towel so it lasts and is ready for a meal at a moments notice. Are the fruits cleaned off before you put them away? A bath of vinegar water for all fruits with permeable skin can greatly increase your chances of picking it up and immediately being able to consume it without a thought or care, you actually save time instead of washing each item before you eat them. Not to mention removing other hands and germs increases peace of mind and immunity. Getting off pesticides and particles from transport gives the fruit back its vitality and you are offered the chance to freely choose these foods and use them more often because you have prepared and nurtured them beforehand.

When buying foods in bulk like rice or pasta, do you put it away in a fresh seal jar that you love or do you just toss it in a pile in the pantry? Storing these foods in a neat and practical way so you can see all you have to work with is the best strategy for being on top of you food game. Its recommended that you search the second hand stores or ask friends if they have jars or containers they can donate to your cause. Keeping things inexpensive by transitioning slowly is the best practice— no need to rush out and spend all of your hard earned dollars on replacing everything in your house that meets this description. As you find a jar, you then decide what item it will hold and you can empty these contents with loving words and kindness, seal it up, and allow it to sit until you are ready, you've already spoken your beautiful words and it is properly being stored, air tight and safe from the contaminants and spoilage that occurs when foods are left in their original packaging.

The point in the process where you begin washing and putting away your precious foods and where you give your food the gratitude and awe it deserves is when your life begins to open up just a little more. When you speak to and are in admiration of the things you consume, the items that truly feed you and they are expressed out loud, you then add another layer of energy to the food you consume. It goes from a completely disconnected state because you may have not grown it yourself, however you insert the love into the food you purchase– you are making a connection by asking this food to nourish you and it wants to deliver.

Take for instance Dr. Masaru Emoto's experiment with water is the basis for understanding just what our words can do to the fluids or foods we consume. In his experiment, when speaking words of kindness to glasses of water and observed through a microscope, the water particles had aligned themselves into beautiful looking snowflake formations that demonstrated absolute perfection and a sense of overall health. When spoken to with nasty/bad words and told things that were not positive, the water displayed a very different outcome through the microscope–distortions and what looked like genuine sickness of the water's cells. This has been replicated many times over as people all over the world put plants, or pieces of food into bowls and conduct the love/hate experiment on their own. Unanimously the results always point to the same things. When the food or plant was nurtured told it was loved and appreciated, it lasted much longer. When it was spoken to with words of hate, the food spoiled or the plant died at rapid rates. Practicing this on your own could not only make your food nourish you better, but make you a fully connected and present human being when it comes to what you put in your body.

This is the intelligence of natural, whole foods and its network of connections to instinctual humans, we know what's good to consume and what could make us feel less than optimal. We know how to give blessings to our foods through prayer, placing it on valuable wears, or decorating it in a way that pays homage to the beauty of color and creativity by accentuating its visual appeal. We can tell when a food is fresh or when it has a small hole because a bug decided to let you know that apple is the sweetest in the bunch. Its not perfection, its allowing the foods to speak to you by the way it looks, your observation of additional things it needs like washing or cutting off insect love bites, its noticing what has true nourishment and what is just another bland, polished and perfected piece of food that looks good, but doesn't feel good.

How You Display Your Food Matters

Now that you've decided to repackage and replace empty expired foods you may decide now how to best display them. Being that food is our direct connection to healing and nourishment its makes sense why we could consider it to be medicine– to be used to best serve the needs and deficiencies we find ourselves experiencing. When you consider medicine in an herbal shop or vitamin store, they have each item neatly packaged and placed like a pharmacy on each shelf. Everything is properly labeled, possibly alphabetized and clearly marked as to how much left of the medicine is left in the bottle. How can your kitchen become your personal pharmacy? Are your vitamins and herbs co mingled with your foods or shoved away in a bathroom medicine cabinet? Do you have space to create shelving so your rice and beans can be displayed in plain view? How about cupboards, are those places that can be refined so you may display your foods in a way that shows you abundance and order?

When your food items are displayed neatly like spices, herbs, vitamins or medicines we clearly start to define that everything we consume needs to have its special place and given the care needed to not only get the best of what that ingredient has to offer, but the chance to shake it up and introduce diversity in the diet daily. More often we consume the same things over and over because its in the front of our sight, we get lazy and have no creative motivation to make something new, or we crave the 1 important ingredient found in that medicine we always consume and we have no other source for satisfying what the body needs. Having 2 different sources of grains instead of relying solely on what rice has to offer is a good practice to follow, introducing other grains like oats, quinoa, barley, or grits can off the bat give you an inexpensive way to keep diversity in your options, but also valuable nutrients as well.

Herbs & Spices As Medicine

We all too often find ourselves eating things that have no real pizzaz, we eat out so often that we consider fast food or restaurant flavor to be the rule and authority. A majority of us don't realize these foods are created to satisfy the masses, not our particular needs, tastes, or cultures. We may not have been taught how to utilize the special herbs and spices available to upgrade our pallet, but often times the experience of having a rich and aromatic experience with food. Our senses can be enlivened by spice making our nose run, warming up the metabolism, and the ability to heat up the body. It feels healthy for some people to experience this every time they eat so they use various spices to give them this feeling such as ginger, black pepper, cayenne, chilli power and mustard. Below are a list of not so common herbs and spices to introduce your pallet to that which not only increases your overall wellness by receiving the nutritional benefits it has to offer, but the permission to experiment with these spices and seasonings to see how they work for you— see if they enhance the overall experience and enjoyment food gives.

Anise- Aniseed, is the fruit of an anise plant and is known as one of the oldest spices, one of the most beautiful too when found in its whole form— a star. Ancient Egyptians and Romans believed this spice to have renowned medicinal qualities. When ground, it is frequently added to cakes or holiday dishes.

Cloves- The word clove comes from the french word *clou,* meaning nail. It can become an easy staple that gives cinnamon extra intensity and gives Chai Tea more sweet and pungent aroma. In a tincture form, this medicine can instantly take away tooth pain. Found quite often in pickling, baked goods and sauteed vegetables.

Coriander- A basic ingredient to Indian cooking and has been unearthed in ancient Egyptian tombs and Babylonian writings. Its an essential flavor in pickling, sausage making, cookies, candies, roasts and soups– really the list goes on as you sprinkle this seasoning and realize it enhances the flavor of the dish.

Cumin- Considered to be an Exotic member of the parsley family, but has a hot and bitter flavor and adds enormous depth and dimension to any savory/umami dish.

Dill- An aromatic herb where its name is derived from the Norse *dilla*, meaning "to lull to sleep"– originally given to infants. Early colonists used this seasoning to stave off hunger during long pilgrimages or church services. Amazing over potatoes, added to eggs, pickles, salads and exceptional on fresh baked bread.

Marjoram- A native to the Mediterranean sea and has been long cultivated as a flowering herb. Used not just as a seasoning but to add sweet aroma and perfume to a room. When smelled, was considered a symbol of happiness and a charm against witchcraft.

Sage- Dried grey and green leaf grown all over the world. In the 16th century it was revered as a symbol of wisdom. When burned it can cleanse a home of negative energies and reinstil a sense of peace and tranquility.

Savory- An herb ancient Romans thought to be the most beloved of the gods. Helps enhance the subtle flavorous of meats and adds depth to soups, stews and sauces.

Turmeric- belonging to the ginger family, grows in the ground and has a vivid orange color. Naturally a sweet and spicy flavor that is mild and inflamation reducing. Great in soups or dishes meant to heal and nurture a person back to health.

While this is just a small list of herbs and spices, you are encouraged to seek out ones that are new and wake up your senses when you smell it. The idea is to realize that variety has an added benefit past just flavoring your food, like times of the past, they were considered and revered as the best things you could put in your dishes. Its what makes chefs in the home and creative artists that share their gift of cooking with people that love them. Share the honor of heightening the senses by opening up to the world of spices and herbs to add medicinal qualities to your foods.

High Vibrational Home & Cleansing Practices

Creating a home that feels free and clear is an art form anyone can learn to practice on their own. Here we will teach you some essential practices that clear stagnant energies from your home, to help compartmentalize certain areas to focus on first and to reduce the anxiety around adapting your physical surroundings to the new state of mind you wish to have. Firstly, you are not required to spend any money for these practices, likely you have some of the things used lying around your home waiting to be used. Some of these methods come from yogic traditions and ones learned through Esoteric practices and can be understood as a "ritual or ceremony" that asks the higher powers that be, for help to cleanse, clear, and purify the area you live in— an open invitation to allow the mind to wander and discover. Visual and energetic freedom of the mind is to exercise its creativity and access to options.

This works with the Kundalini and the 7 chakra's because it allows the energy centers to rotate and evolve through the places and activities you spend the most time. When your vibration is high it means you are an attraction to positive interaction and deflection of ill will. Conversely, if your vibration is low it can be felt as a gnawing negativity constant feelings of lack and discomfort. Anything you can do to increase the energy of your spaces is just one more chance to get to the higher realms of your consciousness and happiness. If you don't do it because its just not something you do, then please open up to the practice of doing it solely to keep your energy centers aligned, your vibrational frequency high and to maintain the opening and release of the Kundalini Shakti within you.

Like stated in your sleeping practices, its imperative that you try your best to rid your space of clutter and unnecessary things that no longer have a sense of purpose or connection any longer. Remove any impediments from entrances or exits that do not allow for a free flow of air to move thought it. Reduce the amount of items sitting around that don't have a proper place, or slowly start to create the space needed for these things to be. Coats hanging off the back of couches or shoes underneath tables only adds to frustration and looks of being unkempt. What's really occurring is the energy of your entire day, or at least when you were out wearing that item is now lying around your house. Whether it be favorable or unsavory energies you experienced with that item, its best to put them in the place of items like this– each area can be focused to a sole purpose or place based on what it was used for. Items that have been taken around town need a proper place and all of the items with that energy need to be grouped together.

Shoes, backpacks, purses and jackets along with keys, sunglasses and masks all need to be kept in areas that are easy to reach, but are understood to be covered in the energies of the places you took them in. While they are not bad energies, they are busy energies and having that business anywhere near an area that needs serenity or connection with others is a recipe for disaster and distraction. Clean clothes need to be away from the dirty ones, do not keep them in the same closet– a bathroom is a better place. Your shoes should be left at the door. Keeping shoes that have walked all around town are essentially covered in dirt, grease, dust or grime. It's a great idea to keep these contaminations off of the floor you'd like to lay flat on, where your kids rest and relax, or the place where you play and wrestle with the dog. These are sacred things you are able to do and keeping this space as clean as possible without shoes is one of the best practices.

Conscious thought about the chemicals you use to clean your home should be considered a bit going forward. Firstly you want to reduce the amount of products that do a specific thing. Bleach is an amazing disinfectant and when mixed with 50% water and a few drops of essential oil, you create a sense of clean and actually clean your space exceptionally well. Vinegar and water is another great solution for cleaning windows and disinfecting surfaces. Running a hand over an area cleaned with this solution is bound to notice its squeaky clean effect. Lastly, there are alternatives to things that clean toilets and showers, one is Borax and the other is Citric Acid. Both found naturally on earth, these items can create the paste like substance and abrasive qualities you may be looking for. There is no need to spend money on the expensive cleaners or "natural" marketed soaps, if you do invest your money on anything, grab another book that has recipes for natural cleaners, you'll save yourself thousands over the long run while reducing your physical contact with things that are not a part of nature and not naturally found.

Scents, Herbs, & Resins That Clarify Your Space

One important way to soothe your senses and to give yourself permission to relax is by utilizing mood enhancing scents in the form of oils, resins, herbs, candles and incense. All of these can create an ambiance that makes your space smell nice, it gives a burnt offering to your purposes in life and helps clear the space you burn it in depending on the intention put forth.. Lets first focus on the ways you can get particular scents to use, how to use them, and the most affordable options for beginners. It is recommended that you take this as a stepping stone or beginning by continuing to study this vast section of healing and peace. Get creative in the ways you utilize scent to improve the quality of your life and take stalk of your spacial frequencies as you move along. Soon you will be able to tell without a doubt that energy in your house needs refreshment and revitalization and this is one of the quickest ways to get there.

Essential Oils

These popular and widely used infusions can be found in just about any store, from drugstores, grocery stores and every big box store chain that sells bedding to clothing. Its not hard to see why its popular and highly supported by main stream stores and online outlets. It adds to the ease of getting to them and ability to replace it as well as keeping the price point low because it is not a hot commodity. These are generally tiny amber colored bottles found in many random sections of stores– be sure to ask if you cannot find it in candle or natural health sections.

The means to which you use these oils varies greatly, but one of the best and economical ways is to by an infuser that you plug in, add water, and put a few drops of oil in. It then works its magic through the vapor and the powerful effects of only needing a few drops to feel the effects of. Which can usually be found in a kit with the oils contained. If not, Amazon, Ebay, or any other big box store online can provide you a vast array of options. The price range gives freedom of choice and has something for someone in any financial level so don't be afraid to pick this option first, if you're on a budget. A few scents below are not only easy to find, but are essential to making a person feel whole and comforted in times of need or people who have a difficult time connecting to their senses. None of the scents below are recommended to consume.

Peppermint Essential Oil- A refreshing scent that helps with nasal and chest congestion comfort. Offers a sensation of tingling in the nose and throat canals. Adds a feeling of cleanliness. Extracted from peppermint leaves.

Lavender Essential Oil- One of the most soothing scents you can utilize for comfort as it has an extreme calming effect. An extraction from the purple Lavender flower. Adds an overall sense of well-being and safety. Great for mental health.

Sweet Orange Essential Oil- A great scent for males in particular because it has the ability to calm and amplify joy due to the increase of calming educing hormones. It can provide anyone with an adds sense of joy or happiness. Extracted from the flower bloom of an orange tree. Great for hormonal health.

Eucalyptus Essential Oil- Used in a lot of medicinal rubs, this scent can be recognized and appreciated as a soother of nasal passages and the feelings of a "heavy chest". Extracted from the Eucalyptus plant. Adds a sense of cleanliness to the home and an awareness of internal health.

Candles
This is another inexpensive way to get a boost, candles are widely available just about anywhere and can range from a plethora of different scents. You're encouraged to smell a wide range and

choose the ones you really connect to. It only takes 1 or 2 to warm and brighten the senses. The wick from a candle can be soothing as you focus on the flame, many visualizations and meditations can add impact with the use of a candle. If you are not able to have a candle for any reason, they do have battery operated candles you can purchase in which you recharge or replace a battery to keep it going. A great option for people with small children or in places that don't encourage candle burning due to fire risk . Choose your options wisely based on your situation, but the choices are aplenty. As always practice safety by never leaving a candle unattended. Below are a few scents that you can count on to be soothing and consistent if chosen.

Sandalwood- A musky, soothing and nostalgic smell that enhances feelings of well-being and relaxation.

Jasmine- Generally a light scent to mimic the actual flower that emits an intoxicating aroma of high and low tones.

Fruit Blends- These can be as fun as you'd like them to be, bringing you a sense of overall joy because they can remind you of times where you felt good.

Cinnamon or Spice- These scents can add a very warm feeling to your home, reminding you of holidays and people you love. Can bring of good feelings of family and fun interactions.

Unscented only Colored- These have the power of still providing many benefits and more of a visual and energetic stance than anything else. Utilize the chakra colors in order to highlight the energies you want to magnify and feel– can also be done with the scented candles and their colors.

Herb or Resin burning/Smudging

This is one of the oldest practices in history from the Greek Mythology periods, Egyptian culture, and even biblical reference has been given to their magnificence by elevating and healing one's life. Its how some connect to god, call on spirits, and simply bless and cleanse their home. Its Important to note that you will need a few items to safely use this as a practice such as a shell or bowl to hold the burning bundle of herbs, a really good lighter and the ability to find the herbs or even dried flowers necessary to perform this cleansing activity. Some great ones to start with outlined below will not only make an inexperienced person seem like a pro, but help you quickly learn and embrace the slow process, a feeling of control, along with comfort over your environment and attitude due to this small practice.

Smudging is the practice of utilizing the smoke from these herbs, resins, or dried flowers to call for specific energies and clearings in every space in your home by dowsing the space with the aromatic smoke rising from its lit cherry. This process is used to clean a whole house, to cleanse ones personal energy and body before a practice, or to offer a specific prayer to someone you love.

Sage (slow growing bush & herb)- Traditional Chinese healers, Ayurvedic physicians, healers of ancient Greece and Rome have all utilized sage as a healing botanical. Not only can this be consumed as a spice for added benefit, when bought in a bundle from a good source, you get the added benefit of exhaling the scent and allowing it to encapsulate the delicate fabrics in your home for a few moments. Usually used in conjunction with a bowl so the ash has a place to go while you either walk around your house to cleanse or you allow it so sit next to you during a meditation or visualization.

Palo Santo (special wood)- This wood is getting increasingly hard to find and those on the market begin to flood the mainstream area's of our lives. When burned it has a wonderful aromatic smoke that emanates from it, usually needing a bowl or special tray to hold it and allow it to burn freely. If you obtain this special wood, take care to where it comes from and its original source, order enough for yourself to reduce your footprint and use wisely so it lasts as long as possible. This can help change the current system beginning to resemble greed. This acts as a barrier for unwanted energies that are of malice or ill intent, increases the energy and cleansing abilities of a space or object.

Frankincense and Myrrh (resin)- An ancient and biblically referenced resin burned to purify and pay homage to Jesus or biblical study. Expensive in nature but goes a long way due to the way its used. The resin comes in the form of a sticky substance that is put into a safe bowl or burner. It is then lit on fire and the resin begins to gently smoke. Musky, nostalgic scent of deep woods and soft flowers. Learning more about this practice can offer some real benefits to those who want to create more ceremony for themselves.

Again, it is recommended that you investigate further with your nasal pallette— essentially, what works for you and your body, allergen levels, and particular likes and dislikes. When you choose scents that are right for you, the only thing to do next is to pick the source you'd like to find it in and the way you'd like to use it and practice with it. There are many more options and ways to indulge the senses of smell. Trying them all is of great benefit as all of them provide a different essence, but all in all this process mimics the utilization and ceremonial properties of the fire element and its intoxicating, cleansing abilities.

When you want to create a ceremony, it's a matter of thinking or saying out loud what you'd like to happen with your full and complete intention behind it. Asking your higher power for guidance and giving thanks to the fire/energy that lights or supports whatever method you are using is essential. No need to worry if it works or not, you will be the judge as you move throughout your days less attached to the outcome, but watching it unfold. The more connected you are to the greater picture and less defined by the personal goal, the easier this energy can work with you. By asking for things personally, you can ask for them on a global scale, in addition to asking for safe passage or communication with the people you love. Recognize this is your power to do, it is not a foreign craft, its ingrained from parts of your ancestry– not of religious or particular practice. This is only to keep you connected to your divine ability to manifest with your words, intentions, and the use of the elements.

Example of a blessing to use

This is a short example of what a blessing, offering, or cleansing ceremony can have. You are greatly encouraged to use your creative skills and personal/global needs to use as your frame of reference. Above all, have fun with this, there is no right or wrong way, only that it comes from your heart.

> "Thank you to this day, thank you for this life and thank you for the newness I am shown. I humbly ask for a cleansing of my space and to manifest only what's meant for me."

NOW YOU MAY LIGHT OR TURN ON YOUR MEDIUM and move freely with your day.

CHAPTER FIVE
Additional Tools For Increased Results

This section is to remind you of your capacity to choose. The choosing is decided by what works best for who you are, how you function, and how to best serve your needs. This book is to provide a guide to the many things you may already find valuable and expand on them or to help you see how simple some of these practices can be and how effective they are to helping you reach success in your journey. These added tools for reference is to offer another way of self contemplation and yet another way you can digest, dig up, and transmute old thought patterns and activities. As mentioned in the previous chapter, these tools are provided to give additional ideas and places as to where to increase vibrational frequency.

Knowing that you participate in a lot of these activities, you are invited to refine and expand these processes by adding another dimension to their meaning and influence in your life. Having multiple ways to digest your emotions and what's happening to you as your life starts to blossom, not only accelerates your ability to awaken from within, but gives you a logical and reasonable approach to what you may be experiencing. In no way are you being asked to change what you currently use these tools for, its merely a suggestion to and awareness on how you can insert more spirituality in a practice you already participate in.

As intense feelings arise, at a moments notice, you have the tools at your fingertips to help you change the frequency of the way you feel. When you are able to effectively help yourself through the hard times in life through these simple yet loving and effective practices, then you start to realize the larger perspective. When this occurs you start to react less to chaotic times of stress, depression, and over-reactivity. It doesn't happen less per se, but what lessens is the emotional connection to the event and the increased ability to remain unchanged or the finesse to effectively solve the issue due to having a level headed approach. So in actuality, it does happen less because your awareness and connection to it has vastly improved.

This is a domino effect of small baby steps, please in no way think you should achieve results like this overnight—which is a relief, you have plenty of time to get their and the closer you think you get, the more you realize there is so much more to explore. A never ending adventure of discovery and self-mastery through awakening is a continual journey. You always create new ways to react to situations and shape the way you want to live as a result of observing how you want to feel on a continual basis. You may soon come to realize you will no longer participate in certain beliefs or routines that don't align with the way you feel.

Journaling & The Questions That Lead To Realization

Are you a person that likes to journal or a person who has in the past recorded the events of your day or the feelings of a particular part of your life? Are you not sure how to journal, how often and for how long to get the most effects? This section of the book offers a little more information on the importance of writing down what comes up for you and some of the best ways to do it so that you have resonance and connection to how you feel and why you are writing it down.

Journaling is a practice that has gone back to the first signs of us being able to catalogue and write down events, including the petroglyphs and ancient markings in the caves of many protected monuments. Journaling 's importance is not solely on the type used, as there are many variations, but the record and the honor of being able to peek back in on time to see where you were and how you have progressed. Patterns are easily seen through the process of Journaling as you realize a lot of what you think about and the things that are important to you revolve back to similar themes.

Have you ever gone back to read what you wrote just a year ago? Is it too painful to go back and look at undesirable times? Its fair to feel this way and you are encouraged to follow your heart, but you are also encouraged to face the changes you seek to find in whatever ways you can, so long as you feel safe enough, have the support of others, and ready to embark on what it brings up for you. However you don't always have to go back and read what you wrote.

Some people use this space as a brain dump where everything that is thought at that moment is spilled on the page or written in electronic form and is done until a person feels done. A lot of these writings can be nonsensical and can also be very intuitive depending on how you look at it. This practice really allows the mind to go while you are often writing words before the words are thought about throughly in your head. This is a highly sought after practice as many practice it daily.

Some use bullets, catalogue each event as it unfolds or gives an emotional upheaval of how they feel about their day, however if you were to go back you would realize it doesn't really have much sustenance. There is no logical connection between the way you feel and the way you want to feel or where the feelings even originally came from. There is no recollection that the occurrence of feelings could be from a subset of emotions from childhood or traumas we have blocked out of our minds. The idea is to visit a new approach as you try and connect the dots and make sense of what is happening in your life instead of allowing it to be a reoccurring set of experiences that never seem to get solved.

Journaling should be saved for your most personal thoughts and feelings instead of a place for your to-do lists or research on topics. No matter what way you do Journal currently, it is recommended that while in spiritual pursuit, your journal be kept private, sacred, and a place for spiritual awakening to happen. Writing down the way you feel is a cathartic process as logic is assigned to the feelings that arise in a person when they sit still enough to investigate and take the time to write about it. It's a level of progression some people forget to incorporate, often wondering about dates and times they came to a realization only to come to the conclusion that they don't catalogue and cannot capture where things were at a previous moment in time. It is highly recommended that you journal after one of your selected practices in SECTION 3: THE PRACTICE & THE JOURNEY where we outline how to take notes on each experience and one that you hopefully participate in daily. Having a separate

Journal or notebook to take down what is occurring for you is recommended.

The Questions That Lead To Realization

As you discover more about Journaling, it might be helpful to use the following questions and or contemplations to allow your mind to extend itself to new thought processes and a possible new way of being. Start by writing out one phrase and then following it with your interpretation and seeing where it goes from there. You might come to some grand epiphany you possibly realized long ago or now you are emotionally fit enough to make the connections. Whatever questions you decide to tackle, know your courageous nature will guide you to what's best, never push yourself past safety and being your own best friend during this time is of great benefit to your psyche.

What is the larger purpose of my life?
Do I have a soulmate and if so, who would they be?
What is a spiritual partnership and what does it mean to me?
How many times will I do this before it catches up with me?
Im not sure I like who I am right now.
How do I change this circumstance, I cant live like this anymore.
What does it mean to me to be awakened?

I have nothing holding me back in life, where do I go next?
I know there is more to life than this.
Do I believe in God?
I want to know more about the meaning of my life and the people in it.
What am I willing to do to achieve my goals?
How do I become more spiritually grounded and mentally fit?
I just went through a major loss in my life, what will help me?
I am attached to things id like to learn to let go of.
There aren't many people like me, why?
When I am by my self I feel...
When I am in a group I feel...
I need more self esteem, but where does that come from?
When will I finally feel content in life?
What's the end goal?
I don't like the people that surround me, but Im not sure why.
My life feels like its falling apart or is.
When I take a risk I feel...
When someone disrespects me I feel...
I am no longer willing to...
I love myself because...
I am lovable because...
Other people love me because...
I feel satisfied when...
I feel joyful when...
I am in gratitude for...

My biggest hope is...
My body is strong because...
I am healthy because of my dedication to...
I am ready to begin a new chapter In life.
I am ready to shed the old me, never to return, what would that look like from my perspective?
I am willing to sacrifice... for my goal to...
I am thankful to my past lovers because...
I have learned from past relationships that I have the ability to...
I give blessings to the people I no longer am in contact because...
I need to break contact with...so that I can...
What's my most unhealthy habit and why is it that way?
I invest in myself by doing the following...
What does giving myself care (self care) actually mean?
My favorite people are...
My relationship to death is...
I am not limited by my circumstances because I believe...
I am grateful for my means of transportation...
I am willing to take a bus, train, or plane to get to...

This list of inquiries can get more elaborate as you start to discover within you what you want to know, if you listen, you will hear the answers and poking around with these questions sparks a conscious relationship with your inner self. You create a language with the way you perceive the world in front of you as you get real with the world you are trying to leave behind or recreate. This work is never without a lot of effort and its no walk in the park. People who embark on the practices throughout this book receive a better rubric for how to get closer to a meaningful life. They also develop the strength needed to carry on as life produces the scenarios required for us to rise up. There is no particular ending to this strategy, only that it can become your next best friend, Journaling as a place where you talk about who you are to the new parts of yourself and together you make compromise on what should stay and what should go so that you may join the new reality of who you are becoming. To walk into a stable life of happiness and to feel prepared to take on life as it comes– to go with the flow so to speak.

Music: Keeping Your Vibration High With Harmony

What kinds of music do you listen to? When you listen to the words of your favorite music, what is the overarching message of what you accumulatively listen to? There is no one way it should be, but take note that if your music revolves around heartbreak, leaving and never coming back, or being cheated on, its an energy that is bound to keep repeating in your life. Words can be spell bounders, in other words when we speak, sing, or intuit words of intention, we tend to manifest that which we focus upon. Its not that we need to be afraid of everything we say and think, but when we do, we start to see the contributors to our continual experience of disdain or disappointment.

As you will see in Mantra Yoga, the words you chant on intently with conviction, words that you memorize that come from the heart and contain emotion will get you closer to the truth, a realization of God, or the opening of the heart & throat Chakra's. If Mantra can go that far to improve your life and give you a practice of devotion, then cant the music you sing, memorize, and listen to over and over have the same effect?

The idea isn't to revolutionize everything you listen to and force you to listen to types of music you do not connect to, but you are invited to discover the recommended genre's to see if they increase your ability to get deeper in your meditative practice, to write for hours in your Journal, or to make an intentional meal from the heart. Its to remove the thoughts and emotions from the music you're currently relating to and allow your hearing a new experience so that it can help move you toward actions you truly desire. What is recommended are genre's you can easily find on Pandora, Spotify, iTunes, or Youtube which all have the capability for you to listen for free.

Genre's to consider listening to:

Anything without words (recommended), sounds of nature, movie soundtracks, singing bowls, Tibetan monks, Yoga playlist's, Kundalini Yoga mantras, binaural beats, drumming, and classical music. You are bound to find something to spiritually connect to in these genres so have fun and remember to click around and listen to as much as you can. You'll be blown away when listening to them you come to a realization doing the same activity however having an elevated frequency due to the music you are consuming.

Nature's Contributing Factor

One of the most important things to nurture is your relationship to nature. One of the only things that gives us a sense that there is a larger force at work is by being in and observing nature. Whether you love to go to the park and sit on the bench people watching, or you regularly go on hiking trips with friends on the weekend, it could also be as simple as a bike ride or walk in your neighborhood as you admire the beautiful things you see. It could look like sitting in your backyard or balcony admiring the birds in the sky or clouds moving by. You likely want to connect to it by touching, standing barefoot, or engaging close to the ground so the Earths natural rhythms help you become more aligned in the process.

The method is to get in nature, to be still and to allow the free forming energy of open space speak to you and allow you a moment of freedom. It helps instill a sense of beauty for the things growing, the children laughing and the grass that is impeccably green and lush. Its noticing how the seasons feel on your skin and understanding by the way the wind blows, that a storm is nearing. Connecting to nature in this way polishes your intuition, gets your body out of controlled air spaces and into the reality you feel, taste, touch, hear, and smell.

So often we get wrapped up in our lives by getting in and out of buildings and cars all day never getting a chance to soak up what the day has to offer. It has become quite a luxury to enjoy any part of your day outside of the realm of work and a weekend. These places further leave us as specters out of a window longing to be out their, but knowing you must be in here, in this building, in this place I earn money to eat and pay bills, it seems hopeless at times for many. What you will come to realize is the opportunity to get out and experience life outside your four walls becomes wildly accessible when you are doing your personal work, giving yourself more freedom and start to manifest the hopes and dreams. If you make any amount of time to be out in nature on a consistent basis, more of it will come as it increases your frequency, gratitude and openness to the larger forces of life.

Community Participation & Support Groups

What many people may not realize as previously stated, this journey is not to be taken alone. While some people in life end up going this route, its not a route for everyone because we all have a different life experience and perspective we are working with. It's not okay to assume that everyone can get from A to B in the same fashion, hence why we have so many Religions in the world—there is no one way to get the Devine.

Participating in a community brings added understanding one may not have while going along on the journey with no one to connect with. Its being able to listen to another persons reality of what they are experiencing when trying to awaken the Kundalini and bringing in some sort of normalcy around talking about spiritual advancement in our advancing technological age. It is recommended to search for closed and private communities that are free on the platforms you already participate on. If you do not participate in social media groups, Facebook is established enough to help you find a spot to enjoy, while Youtube provides a vast amount of community members with a story to share and a lesson that has been learned. There are numerous forums about the subject of spiritual awakening and the positive effects of stimulating the Kundalini to awaken. Resonance with other people going through radical change such as yourself will allow you the freedom to feel more at peace and a sense of acceptance with what you are embarking upon.

Its also important to stress the need for a physical community of people if it is within your means, location, and comfort level. The reason is you always have a back up of support should the internet not be able to deliver what you need. We all know it can be a place where we are left to be vulnerable, some people feel okay with this exposure and others feel too sensitive to let these things go to the eyes of the untrusted. This is why its important to find groups that are practicing these techniques and to meet in public places where you can practice together and safely interact with one another. It may have to be a retreat, or finding a Facebook group that meets in the park once a month or a book club that conjures at a coffee shop a few towns or even the next city over.

While you may live rurally or don't have the means of your own transportation, it is recommended you plan for times out when you can have these experiences. They don't need to occur all the time, but they do need to be a part of you to enhance your experience of life.

CHAPTER SIX
The Physical Journey to Awakening: Yoga

Yoga means to Yog (to bring union) to one's body and mind with the use of specific physical bodily postures called asana. Asanas meet a body where it is and is the place where inflexibility of the body and mind reside. One does not need to be flexible to practice yoga, in fact, you become flexible when you practice yoga. Little by little you are able to stretch and bend beyond the previous days restrictions. It is through the practice of asana that you learn where you are in life, it leads you to discover that the mind is the main place we reside. Asana enlightens you to the idea that the best physical practice one can have is when the mind is free from the nagging thoughts of "I cant, I wish, and I wont", not how far you can go into the posture.

Yoga also includes pranayama which is another meaning for breath work. Breath work is when the inhale and exhale are controlled in a way to achieve a state of equilibrium. It works the cardiorespiratory response that encompasses the full functionality of lungs, the heart, and blood vessels. Pranayama can be done independently or combined with the practice of Yoga and both provide major benefits. Through the diverse study of yogic lineages, you learn each one does it slightly different when combining the breath with movement, and will be discussed in detail further along in this chapter.

When we reach the point of physical practice and conscious participation with life, the mental process around awakening the Kundalini starts to become one of deep understanding. When changes are felt within the body, we soon take notice and want to make sense of what's happening so emotional connection can be finally reached– when head and body connect. The movements of yoga not only give the body more flexibility and stamina, but they help you reach a state of ultimate connection with the self. It is here that you work with the physical aspects of the Kundalini by using asanas (postures) and pranayama (breathing exercises) to awaken the 7 energy centers in the body.

The Oldest Writings on Yoga

Originally the lineage of yoga was passed down only by word of mouth, from guru to disciple, the practice was protected and only taught to the most devout students. This allowed the influence of the disciple to be that of experiential knowledge from the teacher, and helped deter students from being misinformed and confused about what the path of yoga was to offer them.

Over time the knowledge of these lineages were transcribed through text giving a written record of the long ago practiced revered by many to be the one to get closest to God, the Devine, the Universe. The Upanishads is a text that has 108 teachings, and is one of them most revered to call back upon. Another text that contains value is the Mahabharata as it too has many mentions of the lineage of yoga and its struggles and downfalls in Indian history.

A yogic text that is revered by Hindu's is the Bhagavad Gita, the quintessential yogic scripture maps out the paths of all yoga's, made applicable to everyone in any walk of life. It's a scripture that shows one how to live in the now, and how to have a practical yogic practice. Heavy ideas about what god is, what war means, and the emotional attachment to outcomes are all themes discussed at length.

One last text worth taking a look at is the Yoga Sutras written by Patangali and is said to have been written before the birth of Christ. While only 196 verses, it is the complete path of Raja Yoga– the moral concepts and realization of the self.

The Many Lineages Of Yoga

There are 5 paths to yoga that provide different ways for the practitioner to obtain a sense of peace, balance and equanimity. Each vein of yoga offers a way to get to the same place but through a different means.

1. Hatha Yoga
The Path to Balancing The Physical & The Mental

A majority of the yoga's practiced in the west derive from the main branch of Hatha. Hatha meaning *forceful* or *ha(sun) tha (moon)* and gives meaning to how we approach the practice. We force the body through a set of postures that help define an outcome of peace, balance, upright posture, and an overall sense of health well being to prepare the body for meditation. There are many fables to who actually created the practice of yoga, however one story does remain true– the desperation to spread the message of yoga all around the world was palpable. Many of these yogis coming from the east, arrived to western countries around the 60's with their own version of what their Guru taught them. Each unique lineage folds into a diverse array of spin offs that offer deeper benefit of physical fitness and promise of higher states of consciousness. Below are many forms of Hatha yoga, who they originated with, and how they are commonly practiced.

2. Karma Yoga:
The Path of Action

This is a path walked when the participant is on the quest to heal and help others in the name of the divine only allowing time for selfless work. With this type of yoga you would volunteer your time to a cause without any compensation, just to serve the good and higher will of the human race. This is a yoga where you have to go out into the world and help make things "right", just, or fair in the best ways you can.

3. Bhakti Yoga
The Path of Devotion

This yoga has everything to do with full and complete faith. It is when you release all worry and want of a thing and let it go to God, the Devine or the Universe. Through devotion ego is released as self identity no longer holds value and the practitioner is left with a form of self realization.

4. Jnana Yoga
The Path of Enquiry

This is the ultimate path to knowledge and comes in the form of meditative awareness that leads to inner wisdom— that which is not taught but intrinsically known. Its to transcend the limitations of the mind and intellect to come up with a logical reason to the practitioners experience. While the path is open to everyone who seek it, success of this path can only be obtained by the few.

5. Raja Yoga
The Path of Introspection

Raja yoga is choosing the path of introspection as a guide to the ultimate path of knowledge. The most "royal" of the yoga's teaches the student to release the self from the material and to go within, directing the consciousness inward.

Kundalini Yoga is included in the Raja yoga lineage and the name is exactly as it sounds, it is a householders yoga of self knowledge and brought to the West by Yogi Bajan in the 1970's. The chakra's are heavily focused upon as reaching and clearing these energy centers are the main objective. This is a dynamic practice that combines simpler body movements with breath work in order to achieve an ultimate state of balance and restfulness to get into deeper states of meditation. The asanas of this lineage are vastly different than most because while they look simple, they don't feel as such. In this lineage, it is the belief that when the body has worked through its discomforts and emotions it is actually ready for meditation. Each set of asana's are practiced to achieve a particular outcome.

Each class begins with a "tune in" of prayers and protections in Gurumukhi (Sikh language), followed by a set series of postures, breathing exercises and ends with meditation. Each class is 90 minuets long and is vastly different from one day to the next.

Your teacher will not do postures with you as it is their responsibility to maintain the energy level of the class to be sure the directives are focused. The preferred style of dress for this yoga is loose fitting white, cotton, clothing that allows the body to move and breathe. The color white is used to purify one's energy field with bright, white, light that magnifies your frequency and expands your aura– it is the "color" or absence of color that gives one openness. This yoga is best suited for those who are on a spiritual quest and enjoy chanting and Kirtan (group singing)

One of the best yoga's to practice in order to awaken the energy centers of the Kundalini, but a class may be hard to find– its not as popular in a studio as the others, but can still be found.

What is interesting is the amount of modern yogic paths that have been invented the last 50 years and continue to grow. Below are a few common practices you may see classes for that have garnered success and a strong following.

***Vinyasa Yoga*-** This lineage was said to be brought to life by a Guru named Krishnamacharya. Vinyasa is a Sanskrit word which means " *to place*" and is a dynamic style of yoga that smoothly connects one posture to the next through the breath. Anytime the breath and movement are combined in series it is called a Vinyasa. The breath is what moves you in and out of transition through a specific style of breath called ujjayi or "ocean breath". This low roar of a breath comes from the diaphragm and expressed through the back of the throat and nose cavity while the mouth is closed. The breath is extremely healing and wonderful to hear as the rhythm of movement and connection to the breath quickly enlivens the spirit. This style of yoga can be done in a vast array of settings, tempos, temperatures, and musical arrangements that fit your personal needs of the day. Bikram or hot yoga is a style that is heats its class up to 105F to help burn the deeper layers of fat and open the bodies vessels, muscles, and tendons so deeper stretches can be had.

Typically a person can experience a "flow" defined class where basic Hatha yoga asana's are combined with movement from one posture to the next. You might hear slow angelic music or something that's fun and lively coming out of these vibrant rooms. Classes are typically 45 to 60 minuets long and can be physically and mentally taxing. This practice will definitely get a person to sweat profusely and challenges muscles you have since forgot even existed. This lineage offers some of the best ways to get back to your regular body movements and works to help you engage the proper muscles. Typically after a few months of practice, you will notice body changes to be remarkable and your range of motion will increase over time.

This is a style for any level of fitness, however starting with a regular Hatha yoga class may be helpful to try before getting to this practice so you are familiar with the types of asana you will put your body through. Usually always practiced in a group setting, everyone will move with each posture together and hold for the same amount of time before moving to the next. You may find a teacher offer physical adjustments to assist proper form, but isn't as common as a regular Hatha class. Your teacher may or may not do postures with you while they try their best to leave themselves open for correction or help needed by students.

Ashtanga Yoga- Again in the 1970's after a few yogis arrived in the west from India, popularity around the study of yoga started to increase which sent hundreds of young enthusiastic yogi's to Mysore, India to study and practice the 8 limbs of yoga under its creator, K. Pattabhi Jois. What makes this lineage so different than the rest is that it teaches one to do practice autonomously. In Mysore, when students would take the arduous journey to arrive at Pattabhi Jois' ashram (hermitage or monastic community), they came to realize they would move together in the same room, but at their own physiological level and capacity. Postures are given one at a time for a student to memorize and perform successfully and witnessed by the teacher until it turns itself into a *series*. When a series is performed in its entirety, they are evaluated and then moved to the next series.

You will find this yoga to resonate more if you are an extremely physical person as this yoga has many positions that are not suited for beginners or those who need therapy work on the body. While this is the perfect practice for an experienced yogi, oftentimes students will find a studio they can attend to keep them accountable to their practice and postures, but also satisfying the feeling of being a part of a group while doing it. Day to day your practice will look the same as far as asana, however you will notice that day to day your practice will look different depending on where you state of mind resides. A class will open and close with a prayer in Sanskrit and the class length is from 75 to 90 minuets.

Yin Yoga- To first understand the roots of this yoga we must understand what Yin and Yang actually mean. Yin is the nonmoving, stead, and the non reactive parts of ourselves, while Yang is the challenging movements toward growth. This is one of the most restorative forms of yoga because it uses slow and long held asana's to help the body stretch the deeper tissues and ligaments of the human body. So while other yoga's focus on the muscle groups to stretch and elongate, Yin primarily focuses on fascia, connective tissues of the joints and bones, so the muscles can relax around them.

This lineage was created by Taoist yogi Paul Grilley in the 1970's.

These classes are usually a quiet and oftentimes low lit as a teacher guides the student from one posture to the next. Generally there is no physical contact unless the teacher feels the student would benefit from a modified version of what they were doing. Usually 45 to 60 minuets long, you stretch the deeper parts of your being– soreness during trial is common. This yoga is best suited for those that need a slow and quiet practice that is low impact. People who are over the age of 60 benefit from this type of yoga the most as it helps maintain problem areas that stiffen with time.

As you experiment with different lineages, you are encouraged to step outside of what has been outlined in this book and explore the many other diverse forms of yoga that exists like, Iyengar Yoga, Areal Yoga, Goat Yoga, Power Yoga, Sivananda Yoga, Restorative Yoga, and prenatal Yoga. You will find as you look further that there are still many more types of yoga forming daily and just how easy it is to find a practice that works right for your body and interest levels.

Beginners Methods to Open The Body & Mind

Now that you have a grasp on some of the practices available to you today, lets take a moment to incorporate normal stretching that you participate in that are yogic in nature as you witness how yoga can effect your state of mind.

In a quiet space, stand up tall with feet shoulder width apart. Roll your shoulders back to loosen any tension as you take some long deep breaths. As you come to a stand still bend your knees slightly as you bring your arms up over your head and stretch them as high as you can. Bring them back to your side. Now inhale and bring the arms over head and exhale as you bring them down to your sides. Good, try that 2 more times as you inhale and sweep the arms over your head and gracefully bring them back to your side as you exhale. As you come to a stand still, close your eyes and take a deep inhale and hold the breath, 3, 2, 1, exhale the breath and stay here. What do you feel at this moment? Relief? Do you feel stable on your feet and strong in your legs? As you open your eyes and come back to where you are, you now come to realize that is the way yoga feels as you release tension and increase relaxation.

Here is another method if your body is in need of new sensations or to release feelings of overwhelm. Laying on your back on a flat surface, allow your body time to relax. Keep a steady and even breath as you close your eyes. Begin to wiggle your toes, now moving to your whole foot and ankles, roll them all around, stretching them to their fullest capacity. Now bring your awareness to your calves and shins, how do they feel? Move your way up your body, wiggle your hips slightly, your waist, belly, chest, arms, hands and fingers. As you give the last few moves bring yourself back to center. Wiggle your neck with the use of your muscles, move your chin, purse your lips, scrunch your cheeks, open and close your eyes, wrinkle your forehead and try to wiggle the rest of your scalp. After you've gotten a chance to move every part of your head, come back to a settle center and inhale deeply, hold the breath, 4, 3, 2, 1 and release your breath. Remain still for 3 minutes before opening your eyes.

This method is probably something you do all the time and is a form of ecstatic dance. Put on your favorite piece of music, the tempo does not matter. Gently allow your body to sway back and forth as the music's momentum grows in your limbs. Let the energy build as you sway. Allow the swaying to become a dance. Be wild and free, don't hold back! Don't be afraid to unleash all of your energy into the movements. Release the tension lurking in the corners of your joints, the strain deep in the muscle. As the music fades, bring your body back to a gentle sway. Bring your arms above your head, inhale...

Slowly release your arms down to your sides, exhale.

A lot of what we do in life is yoga, we just don't have words to associate it, we see them as activities that heighten our sense of feeling good. Opening yourself to these simple yet effective methods allows you to see how the feeling of yoga works through your body, the sensations that may wash over you and the variations needed to experience a sense of relief.

Making Yoga Simple & How To Develop A Practice

Making Yoga simple and a part of your day everyday routine takes a new mind set when it comes to putting our body first. Its not throwing your clothes on, grabbing your gym bag and driving down to the place where you follow your autonomous daily routine. No longer are you mindlessly doing something for the sake of getting there, doing your reps, and finishing. Yoga is moving with yourself to see how you are feeling and where you are at. It's the subtlety of knowing that each day is uniquely different, because you wake up to feel angry for no reason and the next day feel elated because the mind feel a little lighter. No matter what way you wake up or how you determine you feel, you do your yoga, and it is what helps you through not only the bad times, but helps elevate the good times too.

For a beginner it is recommended that you try quite a few lineages before deciding on the one you will start your daily practice with. Take your time, there is no rush and consider doing the practice twice before you decide you don't like it, give up, and move on to the next. Its like food, sometimes you have to eat more than once and in a few different settings before you realize you like it– allow the time for it to grow on you. As you move through the many practices you'd like to try, you are encouraged to keep a few in your arsenal, the reason for this is because it feels better to have something else to fall back on should you get bored or need a shake up from time to time.

Decide which one will be your go to, or if you will choose to change the practice from day to day. Remember, there are no rules, if you decide Kundalini is on Mondays, Ashtanga on Wednesdays, and Yin on Fridays after a long weeks worth of work, then so be it. Just keep in mind that particular results are better experienced when the lineage remains the same for at least 40 days– play with this and see what works for you.

Next you'll need to carve out some time from your day that is feasible to do each and every day when you are ready. Starting out, its best to find a time of day where you have at least 30 minuets of open time on a consecutive, daily basis and choose 3 days out of the week to start your practice and participate for no less than 10 minuets each time. After 2 weeks increase it a day until you've reached the amount of days you'd like to practice, whether 5 to 6 days a week or an everyday commitment. When you've reached your max days, you'll then increase the time of practice until you've reached the time you're lineage will require for a full practice.

Experienced yogi's may decide to shake up what they are currently doing by changing their current perception from just a body practice to encompassing a spiritual one. When someone has a daily practice in which they devote their full and complete energy, where they chant on the divine, and choose to do it every day rain or shine, happy or depressed, is called a spiritual practice and has a name, Sadhana. The practice of Sadhana is never easy, in fact it's the hardest thing you will do for the day, and everything else you will encounter for the day will feel downstream. The time of day is important as well, its important to either practice at Gods hour (3-6am) or the Golden hour (4-6pm) as these are the best energies in the sky and when you can connect with yourself the deepest.

No matter where you are in your journey, you are encouraged to take these tips as a starting point for your evolution. Times and days to practice are only suggested for the highest intended outcome and is not a rule of thumb until the test of time. Its much better to adore a practice that doesn't follow anyone else's rules rather than doing a practice you truly hate because there is too much doctrine. Now is the time to start choosing what you want out of life instead of following something that doesn't feel authentic to you.

CHAPTER SEVEN
Opening The Path To Liberation: Mindfulness Meditation

Meditation has records dating the practice at around 5, 500 years. It is the seated practice of sitting down in a quiet space, bringing focus and awareness to the present moment and witnessing what comes up. With many forms of meditation out in the world, the practice of Mindfulness is one of the most popular. Its been adopted by those who want a deeper spiritual practice and also those who want no secular reference at all, both just wanting a connection to the self that is of non judgment. It is said that when one has let go of all thought, the path to liberation opens to you, like Buddha after his enlightenment.

Humans are reported to have more than 50,000 thoughts a day and spend upwards of 50% of our waking state in thought. What an amazing set of numbers to realize that we are in our minds a majority of the time and letting go of thought isn't as easy as its touted. The idea of meditation isnt to get rid of or have no thought at all, its merely an observation of what's happening inside your head and bringing yourself back to the breath.

There is an amazing set of scientific research that proves Meditation changes the structure of the brain. The hippocampus, responsible for memory and learning has been monitored to increase in size in people who meditate regularly and have for a few years. Another area, the amygdala responsible for our fight or flight response, in charge of stress, and addiction receptors in the brain actually shrinks when meditation is practiced on a regular basis. Meditation not only gives you high states of relaxation, but enhances the positive parts of our brain and lessons the negative responses we encounter. In turn, it reduces the experience of depression and anxiety, overtime improving the quality of lives among millions of people. Over 14% of people have tried meditation, right up there with the amount of people who practice yoga, 7% of children have had experience with it, and since 2012 meditation has tripled in the number of practitioners according to Pew Research Centre in 2014.

The amount of successful people in the world that practice meditation is astounding, from pro athletes to Olympic medalists those who perform physically for sport often take moments to meditate before a game or event to increase states of focus and to reduce the amount of anxiety and nervousness. Even corporations are jumping the band wagon in mindfulness as companies like Starbucks, Google, Apple, and Bank of America. That's not to mention the moguls and billionaires of the world like Russell Simmons and Bill Gates who brag about their extensive, never missed meditation practice. This practice soothes people who make decisions in the world large or small.

"In our everyday life our thinking is ninety-nine percent self-centered. 'Why do I have suffering? Why do I have trouble?'"
-Shunryu Suzuki

Identifying Mindfulness Meditation

As previously mentioned, there are many forms of meditation in the world and in this book we will focus on Mindfulness as it is one of the most widely practiced, removed from secular reference and just about anyone with a brain can try it. Mindfulness is noticing the thoughts that come into our awareness and choosing the way we respond to them— by trying not to respond at all. Inevitably the mind is going to wander, even after years of practice you will find yourself thinking about past ideas and current things that need to be done. Its to teach you not to react to this fact but instead give it attention and then take the control back by re-centering the focus on the breath, how relaxed the chest and face feel, and how connected you are to your body in the moment.

To get a better idea, lets take a moment to practice mindfulness meditation together. Only practice this if you are in a safe environment where you are not driving or needed anywhere that requires your attention.

Please sit in a comfortable seated position with the back straight when you are ready. Take a nice deep inhale and exhale through the mouth. Now bring your hands softly together and rest them at your lap, continue to focus on the breath and notice the ease with which you are breathing. Now bring your focus to relaxing the forehead, removing tension from the brow as your eyelids soften a bit. Inhale deep, exhale completely. Continue putting your awareness to your body as you feel gravity pull you close to earth, allowing you to sink in a little deeper as you feel the heaviness of your body. Sit here for a moment as you notice the ease with which you are breathing. As thoughts come into your awareness, allow them to show where they came from as you quietly observe and allow them to pass as you bring your focus back to the breath. Inhale deeply, exhale completely. As you sit here for a few more seconds allow your shoulders to drop just a little more, releasing thought, bring yourself back to the breath. Inhale deeply and exhale through an open mouth. You may open your eyes when you're ready. How do you feel and what do you notice about the state of your nervous system? Do you feel more calm or more agitated?

Misconceptions

One of the largest misconceptions about meditation is that you don't have the time, its not worth it if you cant have a serious, committed, hour long practice everyday. With just a short 5 minuets of sitting on the couch, focused on the breath, you can obtain the benefits of someone who does it for an hour, while the effects may not last as long, you still garner the positive results and with time, favorable effects last longer.

Another misconception is that you aren't supposed to have any thoughts and you're not doing it right if you do. False. To display how hard it is for a human being to control their thoughts, I'd like for you to please close your eyes for a moment and bring your focus to a polka dotted duck, good, now sit here with your focus on the polka dotted duck for the next 30 seconds. Were you able to keep your focus solely on the duck and its spots? Or did your mind wander a few times about why you're thinking about the duck, why the duck is the color that it is, or what you feel like eating next, you've proven to yourself how almost impossible it is to stop thoughts from coming in when you are focused on something intently.

The idea is to understand there is more to it than just thoughts, it's a practice and its something that is exercised daily, not mastered. If it were mastered, would you continue to do it? If all perfection was achieve in life, would you go for anything more?

How To Develop A Practice That's Right For You

Meditation, like yoga, is not a one size fits all approach. Just because mindfulness works for some, doesn't mean you'll like or connect to it and stick with it. Before you let it go maybe consider different approaches that help you achieve similar benefits. While you can practice for an hour each day for years on end, maybe that's not what your life is supposed to look like. Considerations for you should be time allotment, guided meditations provided in this book, or your own seated practice and direction feels more suitable. With the advantages of being an all around better person, why wouldn't we want as many people doing this practice as possible? Any heightened states of being will make you want to share it with the world, or hope that the message is spread across the masses and it is. We all benefit from the 5 minute practitioners to the monks who practice all their lives in the mountains of the Himalayas.

You are highly encouraged to follow the meditations provided in this book as a start to your new practice. In the many, you will find a few that resonate deeply and can grow to feel like something you'd like to do daily.

CHAPTER EIGHT Rewiring the Brain: Hypnosis

What Is Hypnosis & What Are The Benefits?

In Western culture, modern hypnosis is credited as being founded on the research and practices of Scottish surgeon and natural philosopher, James Braid in the early-19th century. Braid was introduced to the work of Franz Anton Mesmer through a four-part investigation of Mesmer's theory of Animal Magnetism written in the London Medical Gazette (Anon, 1838). Originally, Braid considered Franz Mesmer's theory of "animal magnetism" -called mesmerism, to be a hoax and scientifically unsubstantiated. Mesmer's theory stated that by having a patient ingest a liquid concoction containing iron, the metal would then be in the patient's bloodstream and could be manipulated externally by maneuvering magnets over the surface of the skin at particular locations to produce improved health and relieve pain.

In 1841 Charles LaFontaine, a touring practitioner of Mesmer's mesmerism caught the attention of James Braid. After multiple demonstrations, Braid believed that mesmerism did indeed work but that neither the iron laden fluid nor the physical touch of the practitioner was the actual mechanism of healing. He surmised that it was actually during the pre-procedure that the actually healing occurred. After attending and participating in three of LaFontaine's demonstrations, Braid realized that the act of sitting and staring into the eyes of the practitioner encouraged the participants mind to focus then slip into a trance. It was this, not the magnets or iron in the bloodstream that put the participants into the calm, "mesmerized" wakeful-sleep state that we now associate with being hypnotized.

"Lafontaine's technique was a combination of physical contact, mesmeric passes, and eye-fixation.[28] It began with operator and subject facing each other. The operator held the subject's thumbs. Lafontaine stressed the importance of the initial physical contact, and the subsequent operator-imposition of 'mind control' once 'rapport' had been established."-Yeates (2018b), p. 57.

Braid's research and experimentation led him to believe that hypnosis was possible without physical touch, and eventually concluded that one could hypnotize themselves-there was no need for the presence of a hypnotists. By focusing the gaze and attention for a period of time on a singular object or thought, a person could slip into a trance-like state with the benefit of depressed sensory functions.

The culmination of Braid's research led to his using hypnosis as anesthesia during both minor and major surgeries for the rest of his career. Baird worked to have mesmerism better defined and over time mesmerism and hypnosis became synonymous, with hypnosis becoming the common term used today.

Using hypnosis as anesthesia was soon replaced as strong, more consistent pharmaceutical medications were discovered. But the benefits of hypnosis are still as useful today as they have been throughout our human history. There has been a modern resurgence of hypnosis in the medical field, with the practice being used in place of anesthesia when and where applicable.

Although it should be noted that here in the US there is no official governing body for hypnosis and hypnotherapy practitioners. The two largest groups are the American Association of Professional Hypnotherapist (AAPH) and the American Council of Hypnotherapist Examiners (A.C.H.E.). Both bodies have base study hour requirements that they recommend but there is no official licensing bureau. It is best to only undergo hypnosis with a practitioner that is licensed in another area such as therapists, psychologists, medical doctors or counselors. Because hypnosis is added to their already extensive study they are likely to be responsible.

Today, hypnosis is used to help people overcome insomnia, phobias, sleepwalking, drug and alcohol addictions, smoking, overeating, chronic pain, anxiety, and depression. The practice is used to help manage the emotional pain that comes from losing loved ones. It is also used to calm patients in preparation for surgery where pharmaceuticals are not safe or the patient needs to remain awake. Braid's practice of using hypnosis is now called Hypnosurgery.

People have a very specific idea of what hypnosis is and more so what it is not. Although founded on the principle of medicine and used as a proven medical treatment for many years, in the late nineteenth century hypnosis had become a novelty act. Hypnotists in street shows and carnival acts pulled volunteers from the audience, then proceed to bring the poor souls "under their spell" before turning them into life sized puppets.

The reputation of hypnosis being an illegitimate con continued and has played out shows for most of the last century and a half. More recently it has become a part of magic stage shows and televised specials. Hypnosis is not a magic spell. Hypnotists do not pop out from the shadows with a swinging pocket watch and put people under their spell. Participants must be willing and relaxed in order for the process to work- even then hypnosis does not work on everyone.

Reprogramming Your Mental Process

The key that Braid discovered is eye-fixation. By focusing one's gaze upon an object for an extended period of time the participant is brought into a state of trance-like deep relaxation. While in this state the participant or patient is more susceptible to suggestions which is why hypnosis is used therapeutically to help people to rid themselves of negative habits or traumatic experiences.

Although the prospect of someone being about to send you into a trance seems scary, trance-like experiences are far more common than we think. "Zoning out" is the most common trance-like experience that most everyone has or will experience in their lifetime. Whether we zone out while washing dishes or our minds switch to auto-pilot during a boring evening commute- there are moments when our attention drifts and we drift- it can feel as if the lights have dimmed. and we do not know exactly how we have arrived in front of our own house because we do not remember the drive home.

Medically reviewed by Timothy J. Legg, Ph.D., CRNP — Written by Kimberly Holland — Updated on May 17, 2018, Researchers at Harvard studied the brains of 57 people during guided hypnosis. They found that:

Two areas of the brain that are responsible for processing and controlling what's going on in your body show greater activity during hypnosis.

Likewise, the area of your brain that's responsible for your actions and the area that is aware of those actions appear to be disconnected during hypnosis.

While the reasons a person may seek out a hypnotist varies, at the core there is a shared belief that each of us holds an untapped potential in our human psyche that if unlocked may save us from ourselves.

Universally, a visit to the dentist is one of the most hated and feared experiences that we humans go through. Some women would rather give birth again than have a root canal, equating tooth pain to something worse than hard labor pain. Smokers notoriously have a difficult time trying to quit smoking, stopping for a period of time before returning to the habit again and again. Because they have yet to successfully break from the habit on their own, some turn to hypnotherapy in the hopes that implanted suggestions such as repulsion at the idea of lighting up will do what they have been unable to do- remove the craving from their mind once and for all.

It is much the same for many of the reasons people seek out hypnotherapy in the first place. They feel powerless to change their behavior add phobias, anxiety, overeating, sleepwalking- each being an unwanted experience the person is unable to detach from on their own. By seemingly reaching the end of their rope and seeking to change their mental programming through bypassing or removing their cravings- the client looks to hypnotism as the answer to what seems to them an unsolvable question.

Hypnosis in ancient India's history has been practiced by Sadhus, Yogis, and sannyasa for millennia making appearances in ancient texts. As part of Yoga Vidya (science of yoga) that has been practiced in India since Vedic times many yogis practice self- hypnosis during meditation to still their minds. The self-hypnosis allows them to sit in meditation for extended amounts of time, perform incredible feats of strength-and in the cases of protesting Tibetan monks, set themselves on fire without relating to the pain of being burned alive.

Following in a long line of the Eastern Sadhus and yogis, Braid observed that by focusing on an object at a particular height and distance away from the bridge of the nose, and turning the eyes upward and inward a waking sleep-state could be achieved.

Today there are many ways to approach and take part in hypnosis. Trained therapists, physicians and counselors are able to expertly evaluate your needs, then proceed accordingly. Hypnotism is a tool that can be used to help in alleviating unwanted habits, phobias and burdens, with their assistance "suggestions" are spoken into your consciousness when you are at your least guarded and open.

There is also self hypnosis. The practice of staring intently at a candle flame, shiny object or even a picture, are all part of meditative practices that date back millennia, but have traditionally been reserved for highly trained religious and spiritual seekers like priests, Sadhus, shamans and yogis.

The meditative techniques of yoga align with self-hypnosis. By bringing your physical and mental body into calm alignment, you are able to be undistracted by the world around you- especially your own body. The calm detachment that can be achieved is what allows the mind to move its focus away from say, an itching toe to totally being able to drift into a state of hypnotic meditation.

There are chants, mantra (rhythmically repeated words or phrases), videos and songs that can also be used to help center your concentration. These can have specific tones and vibrations meant to achieve the same goals as a hypnotherapy session. But just as you have to be a willing participant when being hypnotized by a professional, you have to be open and receptive to self-hypnotism.

Example Of A Self-Hypnosis Practice:

Turn the lights down in a quiet space away from others or intrusion. Allow yourself a moment to get comfortable in a seated position. Sitting in a chair is fine although sitting with your bottom flat on the floor with legs crossed is the preferred position, but if you find it uncomfortable it will be distracting. At eye level place on of the following: a lit candle where the flame is fully visible, a simple picture or painting with a centered focal point, a brightly colored single flower in a vase or even a charm on a chain. The key here to have the object at eye level (this is more easily achieved by placing it on an end table while you are sitting on the floor).

With a straight back, place your open palms flat on your knees and begin to fucus on the object in front of you. Initially your mind will want to begin describing the object. Oh, this picture of the full moon is great! It really is my favorite photograph, I wonder how the photographer captured such s great shot I can never get that with my phone. Man, i need a new phone with a better camera... and so on. Allow the words to cone fighting against them brings even more focus to your thoughts- which is the opposite of what you are trying to achieve. Keep your focus centered on the image of the moon, eventually your eyes will begin to "cross". In doing that your eyes will lose sight of the edge of the photo, the frame around it, the table that is holding the frame, etc. The blur will become what you actually "see". By maintaining this focus you should begin to "zone out".

Let it be said here, that this takes practice. Even though you may find yourself zoning out from time to time by accident while watching TV or washing dishes it is something that comes involuntarily- a thing we apologize for. Because you are now consciously deciding to do so, it becomes more difficult. You will feel as if your eyes are dry and need to blink, maybe you can hear the ticking of an a clock or the honking of a car horn in the distance- these are the things that keep you from fully releasing into a hypnotic state.

The difficulty in self hypnosis is that you are not able to make verbal suggestions while in the hypnotic trance-like state to yourself. With the help of technology this is easily remedied. There are audio and video recordings that can be listened to while focusing on your object. These are the same type of recordings that can be used while sleeping to implant desired behavior changes in the subconscious without resistance. You can record your own voice repeating the desired goal and positive affirmations that can be listened to while focusing on your object. Or, if this feels difficult, the simple act of taking time to attempt to hypnotize yourself may give you a calming and tranquil outlook on the wondrous powers of hypnosis.

CHAPTER NINE
Healing & Experience

Now that you've taken in the knowledge of integrative life practices and an explanation of what they are and how to simply integrate them into your life mens that over time you will start to notice change or the inclination that something needs to change comes into your awareness. These will come in the form of experiences that seem a little too eery, coincidental, or are pure synchronicity. They will also come in the form of realizing there is healing that needs to take place and paying attention to these areas and their meaning through the system of the chakra's and any outside therapies that may have happened or continue to happen on a regular basis.

This chapter is to offer a practical approach to healing and is in no way trying to put fear or expectation upon your experience. These are only scenarios if they possibly arise and not a definitive reality for your life or future. With all that said, what's important to note is a vast array of things will occur and its good to know about some of them before they feel like something detrimental, something you're not equipped to deal with, or that you're at fault for your experience. Sometimes when things start to fall away, the day to day starts to take on a new shape as priorities and the innate need to have ongoing adventures send you in a different direction than the people around you. When you can take full stock of what is ahead of you, the chances of your preparation, how you tend to and care of your personal needs, and your reaction become another part where you get to go with the flow of life, realizing it's a part of the chain— resolution and peace when someone else experiences tumult, absolute bliss, and all out confusion.

The last thing to consider before we start is your ability to share for the extension of healing to not only yourself, but the people that get a chance to resonate with your story and also not feel alone in the process. At first it might just look like an amazing friend who too, is going though some amazing things in their lives, or it could be a trusted therapist or counselor that you've been confiding in for some time. What this gives is yet another example of what happens when people come together for and in rally of healing one another by offering genuine words of encouragement, a nonjudgmental ear, or an inquiry to know more about who you are and what your reality is. While scary, while vulnerable, the most impact and value you have to give is when this experience is shared with others is to offer a dialogue and heathy digestion— full personal understanding.

When you get a chance to know the why's to an experience and feeling that needs to be addressed you understand at a fundamental level what the larger scope of it was and how it helped in the process of you getting here and inquiring about how to have a better life, how to achieve an ultimate state of happiness that feels consistent and safe, and ultimately rise your level of consciousness with the Kundalini. Try your best to take in this process and to understand that life, just like childbirth could not occur without some amount of pain.

What Does Spiritual Healing Look Like?

Spiritual healing can look like many things. From a visual context it can change our sense of style over time as our values start to become more refined. When people go through an awakening of course they experience a wake up call to what needs to change, but often times it has people undue healthy habits just for the sake of understanding the body's natural process. A person could give up on all hygiene in order to understand what they really smell like. Ridding oneself of perfumes, additives, hair dyes and overly chemical additives in just about everything that's used. A person starts to wonder if there is a healthier option or one they can make on their own. Allowing the natural process of the hair to grow on the body is another popular and visual cue that things are stirring in the mind. Anything from long hair, beards, no shaving of any kind for any gender. Make up and products added to the hair start to transform into their natural versions, possibly giving a person a sense of relief from being bound to that way of hygiene, as there are many.

Another visual representation of what spiritual healing looks like is a persons association to material belongings or "stuff". People who go through Kundalini Awakenings report to have experienced the life of having it all before it being taken away for a more humble experience. You go from having matching furniture on credit, the newest cars, extra non used bedrooms in the house, and regular nights of eating out to something less taxing on the resources and metal space to keep up with it. What it first looks like to other's these days is an extreme case of minimalism where you get rid of everything and only own what you can fit in your backpack and others think maybe something is going on with you and you need someone to talk to. Whatever the assumption the only thing that's happening is a disconnection because they do not have the same realizations as you. They could possibly still be attached to everything they own, unwilling to get rid of any of it, constantly buying new and recycling old as if nothing can be used to its full capacity. It's the potential to not be aware of how the habit of keeping these things no longer provides value and it may be time to assign it to someone who could have it in that way.

As you get closer to your inner self, closer to the awakening of your full capacity items around you start to have a different value— you remember its something you loved as a child, but lost along the way. You start to render the items that you do keep as valuable and contributes to your happiness starts to take on a new look. You take the time to refurbish them, clean them, resole them or give them a new re-purposed function. If you do shop, you shop for the best quality you can afford so it lasts. Loving something that lasts is a wholehearted experience that is getting lost with time due to quality of products lacking due to cost. Utilizing natural products or byproducts of natural resources that already occur such as wearing leather or cleaning with vinegar is what keeps you continually bonded to the practice of knowing what's in a product and how that garment may react with your skin because its allowed to breath and is free of synthetic fiber.

What it can also look like is the "disappearance" of your friend, wondering where they have been, why they have been distant or why they no longer reach out. Bare with people as they too get used to your new situation and try their best to cull all sorts of assumptions about what you're going through and what you possibly need. You don't always need to include others in your business if you don't feel its necessary or supportive, but some people do deserve a fair warning that you may take a hiatus. It may cut out that possible chance of receiving a well check from an officer because your 3rd best friend is starting to worry. It can look like a serious cry for help or the suspicion that you should be put on suicide watch. Its pertinent you communicate to a certain degree of what your adventure might look like— you taking a break to go within to see how you feel about things and what you would like to change. Simple, sweet, and still quite private for those who need that safety.

Spiritual awakening can also look like taking on new passions or reviving something you've pushed aside for far too long. There may be a book or piece of artwork you'd like to start working on or a business venture you had been too afraid to take on because the lack of confidence in ability. It can be the urge to finish that project or to take the initiative to see if there is a higher spot in your career you could go.

It can look like an individual who is in love with life and other people as joy starts to consume your persona and speech. Compassion becomes a mainstay emotion as you begin to forgive and let go of situations that hold you to emotions you no longer wish to feel. It can also look like someone who takes responsibility for the way they feel and is emboldened to express that kindly if necessary— you no longer feel the need to lash out, but you certainly will not be treated in ways you dislike.

It does not look like a walk in the park but it also doesn't look like detriment from your point of view as long as you don't allow it to. We would never want to victimize ourselves because we are having a moment with reality, its much easier to try and move past it understanding that above all there is a reason and some higher purpose that may be greater than you at that moment, but in retrospect you usually always get the answer somewhere down the line– it reveals itself if you are listening when you ask.

Symptoms Of Chakra Healing

Symptoms of Chakra healing will be on the account of the body locations and the actions of working with the Chakras as outlined in this book. They are of reality and experience so if it is your reality to have some of these symptoms be sure to take time to rest, always be okay to pull back a little and the smaller steps you take, the less amount and detriment and harm you could inflict on yourself. This is not medical advice, so if things are feeling off because of your changing lifestyle, a previous prognosis, or what really feels like something wrong, please see your medical doctor before moving forward. We can never mask our real symptoms with this knowledge and do nothing constructive about it— we must if we are able and it intuitively feels like a real issue. Its good to listen to your body as much as possible through this process as the removal of toxicity and items that serve no healthy purpose are replaced with the good you are learning to inject, take stock, journal and pay attention to the changes of your rhythms, your breathing, your heartbeat and overall sense of well-being over any amount of time during this process.

The healing symptoms of the **First Chakra** involves the organs connected to the Root of the body as it is in a seated position. This would be the sexual organs and anus— the organs of creation and elimination. With that said, what may occur are things related to this area of the body that may have never occurred before that send a chain reaction to nearby areas as a cry for help to solve the problem. Anything from hemorrhoids, constipation, or pain in the tail bone can be signs this area is experiencing a change. While painful, it usually acts as a physical representation of irritation, inflamation and agitation while internally it's a pain no one can see or feel so its as if you go at it alone.

This could be a time in your life where you question your sexuality or experiment with parts of yourself that have been dormant until embarking on this journey. While some of this may feel extremely uncomfortable to deal with or bring up unexpected memories or reactions in others, you are encouraged to slowly progress, not to fixate on situations that seem confusing— no one else needs or deserves an answer, there is no rush to reach to any point or get to the bottom of it for resolution. There may also be a slim chance you will not deal with it, that you will observe these feelings and your own wonderment about sexuality by giving it honor in your own private way— this is perfectly healthy.

Another experience with this area of the body are the loss of sexual appetite or loss of feeling during masturbation as these areas become less sensitive— your mind starts to focus on things it feels is of greater importance. However this may not come until after a long rapport with other people you have exchanged energy with and are done giving yourself in that way. It may come after a long obsession of sex and masturbation. It may also work the other way around where you might find yourself awakening sexually after a long hiatus and are rediscovering your body. Whatever way you are pulled, you are encouraged to safely explore these areas of your body and possible fantasies that may arise. In the end, what it will always boil down to is being connected to another person or yourself fully as a spiritual person forces those needs and fantasies to reshape themselves as a desire of actualization and real lasting physical connection with a focused energy towards as many as one can handle. Practicing celibacy is a common force and is a surefire way to genuine love and happiness— harnessing and growing your sexual power and health.

Mental connections can revolve around any form of pushing past the mundane and a focus toward an understanding of life that's past the normalcy of day to day routines. This is where a lot get cycled through. Looking around to realize you may have been living in excess or beyond your means is likely and survival starts to kick in— you need new strategies and possibly need to let go of a few things. Mental and physical symptoms can occur simultaneously through any process of working with a Chakra so stay aware of the changes and what doesn't feel like you or what feels like it needs to be changed for the sake of your sanity.

The healing symptoms of the **Second Chakra** involves the organs connected to the reproductive system.

For people with a uterus, where menses and baby growing takes place as well as the surrounding internal organs of the urinary system. This can be removed and still experience sensation as the organs and the space around it has repositioned itself. For people with a penis and sperm producing scrotum, it will also include urinary organs. These organs too can have been removed but still feel the sensations of the area when the energies are being worked with. For trans people, this can really be interchanged so listen to who you are and what your body is telling you. You are encouraged to feel this part out, while the Chakra system has been around for thousands of years, our idea's and values around gender and the body parts associated were not as complex back then as they are now. Feel free to play with this area if you are a person who is exploring their gender or is wanting to connect to the process naturally. There is no right or wrong way, no right or wrong body part to have to make it true– the only truth comes from you.

A physical symptom that may be unnerving is the difficulty to have a painless period if you have a uterus that still has a monthly Moon cycle. It can be increased cramping or the passing of larger things during the moon cycle– the body reacts in this way quite often, by trying to rid itself of old tissues and stored painful memory. When a body carries a baby at any point in life, this chakra is stimulated to awaken automatically, it may not fully, but the opportunity is present. Or for a person with a penis, brief dysfunction can be experienced as well as pain or an unexpected injury. Loss of sensation or libido is a common occurrence and is a symptom of pushing past unhealthy emotional and physical barriers– getting to the higher states of spirituality.

Mental connections can revolve around any form of pushing past old issues and traumas from past lives or in the present lifetime. Issues that arise from childhood are extremely common as well as any parental or familial toxicity that has gone unchecked. Again, because this chakra is ruled by water, emotions are the main focus and achieving emotional maturity can be the highest reward to gain so that advancement can continue. Old conversations that seemingly were put to bed start to reappear as old patters come back to remind you that you still have work to do. This can be some of the deepest mental work because it is the blockages of the 1st and 2nd chakra's that are the hardest to surpass and awaken, but once achieved can be rest assured they will not slip back into the sleep state– where one is asleep to their lives. This is the part of healing that feels terrible to be dealt with, helps us deal with grief and pain through the process of learning how to breathe again while working with the 3rd chakra.

More mental breakthroughs and thoughts that help heal this area of the body are your relationship to children if you have any, want any or never do. It revolves around the relationship to your lineage, ancestry and what legacy you will produce to pass on. Questioning your role in parenting and the desire to be better at it is a common theme.

The healing symptoms of the **Third Chakra** involves the naval and any organs around or behind the naval point. This is the point in our lives where we realize how old or young we fell based on the life force energy or Prana we have in our bodies. Ancient Yogic traditions measure someone's length and worth of life by the quality of the Prana or breath. It is said you are born with a certain amount of Prana and you are to not waste it on activities that take away the health and magnetism that radiates from a person working through the Third chakra. As stated, the Third chakra is the center to which one starts to work with the blossoming of their consciousness, toiling with and clearing, polishing and making space for a new person to emerge. Increased amounts of energy can be felt here, it less sleep than previously required, creativity starts to emerge while self confidence is solidified and boosted.

Physical reactions of healing when working with the Third chakra are first a downgrade of one's immune system as consciousness starts to awaken all the parts of the body that need to be worked with. You may find yourself with a common cold once a month, or drop into a series of issues that manifest as ill health and an important place of focus. This may be a time where you visit hospitals for check ups to investigate phantom pains and ill feelings that you haven't had an answer for. You may find yourself on a medication you didn't know you were going to need and dealing with how that increases or decreases the quality of your life and your immune system in the process. When consciousness awakens so do the physical issues as everyday you may be feeling like you are dealing with yet another issue in your life that has manifested in debilitating back pain or a once a month flu that follows you around.

Symptoms of real stress can appear while healing this part of your life and body, again you are awakening parts of yourself that have been asleep for a long period of time, you are bound to awaken some of these stressors until you realize you have control over your reactivity, and the trickle down of stress starts to lesson as you trust yourself with every progression forward. This is one place where we start to realize that the head and body should be connected and start taking more stock in the physical health we have or lack thereof.

Mental healing will look like a number of questions you've never asked yourself, and you may find yourself willing to act on something you never thought you would, like moving jobs or taking on a new exercise system so you can get your health back. Stressful work out systems or facing the reality of your health situation can also contribute to the physical stress felt, but overtime you will start to build an impeccable response system that is resistant to and has stamina for dealing with stressors.

The healing symptoms of the of the **Fourth Chakra** involves anything to do with the area of the heart and the lungs. Because this place is a sensitive spot due to the emotional nature and comfort with vulnerability that makes this Chakra so crucial. Partly, its full awareness that the heart beats in a continual manner if we are healthy and disease free, for this reason, its important to show up to life and our relationships in the same manner. Experiencing a sense of blockage can occur simply because the heart center is unable to open up and trust others. Fearing that if they expose themselves, it may be used against them in future scenarios and could be a possible experience that happens time and time again pointing you to not close up and mistrust, but to understand that not everyone should be in relationship with you, not everyone can deliver in the ways we desire— and that's okay. This healing has the ability to take you back to areas of your life that need more strength and resource behind them (i.e. home, earning potential, and backup resources). It's a place where we cannot be in true relationship unless we experience it on a deeper level by going at it alone— developing self reliance.

Working with this chakra can physically manifest as a change in body temperature as you open up your blood gets pumping you are using your lungs more, breathing more, doing more, and being more. It is here you see how much resilience you actually posses as you figure out ways to reshape more of your life. Beauty can never be achieved without some form of pain and sometimes that pain is physical as you move and change the energy— please don't be afraid, what's on the other side is more than you could ever imagine to dream. It is also here where some say palpitations can be felt as the heart catches up to the frequency of the rest of the body, like its shocking itself back into functioning. However, if this is associated with pain, and feels irregular or worrying, please speak to your medical doctor to be safe. This is not a diagnoses for a more serious unchecked condition.

Mentally however is when most of the pain begins as these memories get stored within the body– emotions made physical. Pain due to heartbreak, feelings of complete loss, hardship and memories that were never processed. This is where it gets deep, where we peek at the things we have been holding onto that we are fully conscious of. Feeling unwilling to let them open, leave, release, or be nurtured. When we start our physical practices like Yoga we realize these memories are stored in our tissues as we move and take shape of a particular posture to realize, it hurts, then OMG, Im about to cry, but why and for what? This is where you cry, it is the point you realize crying contains cleansing for these emotions that are being carefully dealt with, its one of the softest ways you can nurture them, give them attention and send them on their way. A wise Yogi once said, when you cry, let the tears fall and don't wipe them away, allow them to cleanse you and your soul.

The healing symptoms of the of the **Fifth Chakra** resemble anything that deals with the areas and organs of the body between the ears and the shoulders. Oftentimes this is the breakthrough area we reach where a discovery is made about our ability to hear outside of normal range or logical explanation. This is the place where we learn that our listening skills are lacking or are on point with collective conversation and presence. Here is when we have realized if we have given our power away and when we feel we need to rediscover our voice. Inner truths come out here and unspoken words become alive and ready to step out to face the music. Your beliefs here can become so ingrained that your comfort with the knowledge and practices you hold, that being right, creating conflict or proving a point doesn't overshadow and dominate the ego.

Physical healing in this area can be earaches, intense non allergenic nasal flare ups, or loss of voice. It is here where long time smokers realize there is something that has changed and if they continue to give their voice away by inhaling smoke, by tamping down their emotions, they will never get the chance to fully live and speak their truth. In time they realize its time to quit or they feel ready or compelled to begin the process of quitting. These areas of the body are going through a readjustment period and its helpful to research natural ways to remedy any pain if felt or to use natural methods to help the ears nose and throat expel toxins and mucous. Again, you know if you are sick or if you should go to the doctor to be sure that you are not, rule out all options so you are safe in this process of awakening, adding anxiety, what ifs and long hours on the internet searching for your symptoms can create a lot of unneeded energy.

Mental healing around these areas can help you deal with how you spend your time and where it gets spent the most. You can feel run down and tired by the mundane practices you've kept up with and now feel emboldened to utilize your time in a new way. You start to express these things out loud more often and people start to get to know the real you. This can feel like exposure, you may not want others to know about your life or your journey, but the idea is to try your best. People, whey seemingly nosey are just curious about the changes in your life. The conversation however will quickly turn from either inquiring minds to confusion and silence because these people are not motivated and geared up by the changes you are experiencing. Or they become more interested or divulge to you their feelings or experiences with the same subjects of likes, dislikes and cosmic connections. You just never know, so choose wisely but don't be afraid to risk, open up and enjoy listening to another experience and perspective on life.

The healing symptoms of the of the **Sixth Chakra** involves the head and the middle of the brow. This area deals with the complexities of a humans inner sight. The eye that is closed to the outside world and focused on the intention, purpose and expansion of the consciousness and self-knowledge. It is here where people decide that their devotional practice needs more intensity, longer times and more study and research to connect. There could be an obsessive process to this where you must consume, see and experience everything you possibly can, where most opportunities seem attainable and where hopes and dreams start to take shape visually. This is a place where you utilize the abilities of your intuition and inner guidance rather than the guru's, books, or online personalities that tout what truly works.

Physical healing that takes place can look like increased headaches, unstoppable mental chatter or a complete sense of relaxation and trust. Visualizations could also be an occurrence as you begin to further promote longer lengths of time in devotion so messages can be easily received. You could find yourself easily distracted or start to feel "off" while in large groups of people.

The mental faculties are seriously challenged with this area, you will be encouraged by your internal free will, to redirect your life so you can remain in states of bliss and peace longer. This is where many start to notice their ability to see the future or intuit what people are going to do before they actually do it. It is where dreams start to take on a new meaning as the faces and activities performed in the dreams start to make sense in a conscious way while awake and point to larger themes and connections in your life. Reshaping the way you think and how you perceive your life will become impossible to ignore as you realize a lot of what you once believed has now been replaced with a higher level of consciousness and self awareness. While in the space of healing the Third Eye you may find yourself unable to connect verbally with people because you feel as if you are on a level at first. People will move slow around you, stare at you when you talk or look confused by the way you move. This doesn't stay for long, but as you move around you will either take a step back to reduce this feeling or move forward with it because you don't mind the extra attention it brings.

The healing symptoms of the of the **Seventh Chakra** involves working with the top of the head and connecting to the higher realms of your subtle body. Attaining this level of awakening opens faculties most people are not able to speak on because they haven't reached it. This is the ultimate state of bliss and what most people try to obtain in order to experience Enlightenment like the Buddha or Jesus. By the time most people get here, they forget the place they came from as they have been reborn and directed to serve life in a different way— not many can choose this path, it usually finds them as they end up in some scenario offering advice to those attached to the material world and no connection with the ethereal.

Physically this can manifest as anything and happen at anytime. Enlightenment is said to bring no more suffering and pain, so it might be safe to assume there may be physical reactions at first and then long moments of no pain. This experience could really be so much more and as time moves forward more and more people become enlightened and share the process of what its like. Personal experience with this holds the torch in authority so choose who you listen to wisely.

Mentally this can look like anything, some might say its crazy, some may say it's a heightened level of consciousness and you should be followed and answer questions to other seekers on how you have obtained and do maintain this level of consciousness.

What's most exciting about the last chakra is not really knowing the full potential of what can happen when you reach the level of no suffering. While life happens, your reaction and perception of if has completely changed that there is not semblance of the person that once was. Just a gentle soul that has the sight beyond sight, the desire to be one with the Devine and the ability to share this gift with the many people wondering how to obtain it.

Those are all some of the most common experiences when working with healing the 7 chakra's and how to accept this energy. It's a level of trust within the self and humanity that you continue to progress to the next stages of awakening. Noticing the subtle non threatening changes that occur is one of the most rewarding take away's— you're fully aware of when things shifted and exactly why they are different. Living in a new way, while exciting can still have drawbacks due to backlash from others that don't understand your vision. The following sections will outline how to best approach the situation when this phase of your life turns up and the best strategies for success and emotional health.

Interacting With Family & Friends While On Your Journey

When you begin the process of awakening a lot is made clear in the first phases of your progress, it will feel like an area you know a lot about and you could often express this a lot to the people you are around that are taking a journey in life that is unlike yours. This is the first step to dealing with the ramifications of what other people think about your journey and the process you are following to get there. For some connections in your life, it may be easier to try and to derail your train in order to "get back the person they once knew". These actions aren't exactly malicious, but more a reaction based on the fact that nothing is changing in their lives, or they don't wish for change to occur.

Everyone's motivations in life are different and when we recognize that at the core, we can find compassion with ease when someone doesn't exactly agree with the approach you take. It's to find patience when someone talks about a subject that is vibrational low, ignorant, or just rude, and they're not able to see themselves. You'll start to wonder why they cannot as frustration and disagreements mount as your approach begins to significantly change. Conversations can become more inclusive, possibly more compassionate to other's mistakes or misfortune, and knowing that every person at the core is inherently good. These may or may not have been themes in your previous way of being, but what occurs is a more accentuated form of it.

A great way to ease into the subjects of talking about "what you've been up to lately" is more of a discussion about the smaller parts and less about the whole of the subject, especially if consciousness is not a conversation you've had with these people previously. Its effective and way more connecting when you can say things like, "oh, I've really been trying to develop a meditation practice or I've been reading a lot and getting into my health again." Talking about the smaller approaches to this life is one way people can start to join in on the conversation.

Not everyone will want to take on a journey like this, its vast and encompasses a lot of self-work with many pieces that make up the larger whole of what you are trying to do. It might be frustrating at first to meet people or have the deep conversations you want to because you realize the motivations of others are as different as there are colors in the world. Instead of taking on the frustration about not being understood, its much easier to value what they contribute to our lives. The pieces we can learn to polish that add value to our greater whole. Pick their brain about what they take pride in, like being an amazing mother, entrepreneur, or how they have achieved that amazing green thumb. Talking about the passions and good experiences this person is having.

This is where you start to take stalk in the real connections you have with people and what the conversations now revolve around, paying close attention to how it feels in your body. You may start to realize a stark change in contrast. When you go from drama latent conversations to ones about growth or positivity, you may not be received in the same ways you were, which is okay. You'll have to decide for yourself how you'd like to interact as your evolved approach needs more enticing and stimulating conversation around what's good, how to heal, and how to support one another.

This brings another topic that must be discussed and that is the loss of some connections you thought you had a better hold on. As you start to change, so do the things you talk about. What doesn't change is your connection, if they stay the same, so does their speech and level of understanding. There may be times where you realize there is nothing you have in common anymore. You start to see how the relationship either positively or negatively effects your state of mind and this is something to sit with for some time— we don't want to toss people aside because they aren't having our life experience. Instead again as stated in the previous paragraph, we take stock in the particular value they do give us and engage on that premise.

Sometimes there is no way of avoiding loss as you just loose touch of the people who once had so much fun to offer your life. As you choose new scenarios to participate in, the previous activities may not align with who you are becoming. The temptation, the vibration and lack of connection can have you not reaching out or you may find yourself being excluded in all the fun and games. Being comfortable with yourself and your new found journey can keep you from activities that you feel no longer suit you. Choosing what you have decided to embark on and staying on that path no matter what others have to say is a triumphant approach that will be rewarded in the end. Your relationships transmute into connections that are deeper and more aligned with the activities you participate in as these people tend to be open and like starting friendships— it doesn't have to be a lonely path.

Professional Therapists & Counselors As Helpful Resources

The importance of speaking to someone while on the journey cannot be expressed enough. In the above chapter we talked about the possible lack of support in our current communities due to our own personal change and the lack of change they are experiencing. This points to what you can professionally lean on to get good and sound advice about what to positively do with what comes up for you during this process.

There are mental memories that come about that find their words through journals, repeated mantras in our heads and emotional release through movement of the body in conjunction with these memories. They can be extremely painful to deal with due to the lack of resonance and feeling understood by another human being on a similar path to spirituality. This is where a professional may be able to help.

When looking for someone to talk to, its always best to go through a reference, a friend or asking out on social media for someone in your local area. Picking out of the many could be a recipe for disaster if you aren't connected with someone with someone you know has helped other people like you. Going off of gut instinct is okay too, you will just need to do a little research and conduct an interview for the person before you proceed– you have complete control. Asking questions like, "how can you help me through my spiritual journey or how do you help people deal with trauma?" Knowing that instead of a diagnosis, what you need is a person that can listen and help you worth through the past in present time in a way that doesn't further damage your memory and perception of it, rather positive reinforcement that you are on the journey to growth. Mentioning opening the Third Eye or Awakening the Kundalini may not be terms you want to use initially, you want to be taken seriously and these types of subjects are not regularly studied by scholars or taught in schools of psychology. If they are, they could be demonized by assumptions of character and sterotype. You want to be seen as a rational person understanding your experience, not a person experiencing psychosis.

Many people benefit from healthy healing from a trained professional, especially if you are dealing with specialized traumas that get ignited during this process such as abuse, abandonment, and the mourning of a loved one. These people can most definitely help you help yourself by teaching and giving you the tools necessary to overcome these memories. Specialized therapies are offered to recall or touch on parts of the subconscious brain that helps a person deeply heal and disassociate from the events emotionally, which can be a relief. Try your best not to write off the chance to heal in this way because of past experience, please move forward and find the people that can assist you In healing through logical and thoughtfully trained approaches.

Professional Healers That Can Help

What is a professional healer? This is a person is usually trained in specific modalities that help people go thorough what you are experiencing with a supportive and graceful approach. These are people that do understand the language in this book and in conjunction with therapy can assist in the full blossom and Awakening of the Kundalini. Below is a short but helpful list of modalities that are safe to step into backed and supported by committees, regulatory societies and stringent codes of ethics.

Reiki Practitioners
This ancient Japanese practice train's individuals in the study of healing with the use of touch. Reiki means spiritual healing life force energy, so in essence, this is a spiritual practice of using lifeforce energy and touch to heal the body's ailments. Highly trained practitioners are able to give a treatment often times not needing to actually touch their clients and healing can be done distantly as people can still feel the benefits. What is fundamentally valuable about this healing is that you don't need to believe in anything in particular,

its not a religion or a rigid set of beliefs. It is governed and supportive by a close nit organization and rigorous set of training needed to be called a Reiki Practitioner.

People often report feelings of bliss or complete comfort during a treatment, often feeling lighter. It is a practice in which the patient takes complete control of their physical and spiritual healing by being present for the self when life calls for it. It's a positive way to assist the body through its emotional connections.

Astrologers
Are a part of a larger network of study called Astrology- the study of the planets and their effects on our daily experience- it covers many different linages and approaches to help a person understand their inner workings on a deeper level. A trained, professional Astrologer can look at the day you were born (Birthchart) to see how you are effected by life and how that can shift and align with the current movements in the sky. It can give a person reasons to why they feel the way they do. Sometimes we don't realize how effected we are by the Moon's placement or what makes us tick and why that wont change. It helps to clarify significant areas of our lives and time frames that can give peace of mind and insight into the inner workings of the psyche. It is yet another way you can internally go within to do more self study for self knowledge.

Yoga & Mediation Teachers
Not all people will fall into this category, but some Yoga & Meditation teachers have the insight and training to deeply support someone emotionally while on their journey to physical health and realization. Their knowledge about the body and where emotions get stored is a great way to work with the energy in a safe and supported environment. Some teachers are able to intuitively feel when you need more, they can help you with proper posture and can verbally guide you to better states of understanding. They are fully trained in the understanding of the chakra system as the premise and study of energy in yogic practice.

Sound Healers
These practitioners use the energy of sound to help a person heal the energy centers in their bodies and to help unwind and loosen feelings that have been trapped inside a persons cells. This is the practice of using instruments or the voice to create harmonious tones that allow a person to fully release and relax. This can encompass things like singing bowls, drums, mantra, gongs, chimes and various other instruments that soothe. You can get the benefits of a treatment through a group class, online participation, or a recording while you relax and allow the mind to drift and wander.

CHAPTER TEN
The Gifs of Awakening

What begins to unfold is a connection you may not be prepared for as new abilities start to occur. Awareness increases in an individual who is working with the energy centers of the body and nurturing the process of awakening the Kundalini, making situations and feelings more apparent, a possible unlikely symptom of self work. We want to be sure you aren't overwhelmed or caught off guard with the different ways life can present while walking along your journey. You may not experience any additional "gifts" that you didn't possess before, they just may be largely heightened or advanced. To know that you possess some of these qualities without realizing it can be eye opening. However what you will come to realize is that these gifts are within us all and are here to guide everyone if they are personally ready to accept the responsibility.

These gifts are usually dulled by lifestyles and constantly being "turned of" and automatic with our process to life. Day in and day out we perform the same activities without much thought as to how they should change. In fact, sometimes the only change we experience is cataclysm, when something goes wrong or needs to be fixed, other than that we get to the bottom of the issue just to go bak to the automatic state of doing the same things out of practice instead of being led by intuition and spontaneous action. This book encourages you to change your routine and tap into these senses as you move about your day, seeing if you can create your own change and spark discovery as you listen to your other senses as guides toward ease and safety.

Increase Abilities & Enhance Senses

What we will outline are senses that you will come into as you increase your intuitive abilitties by listening to yourself, going where you are being led to, and doing your practice so that your mind is free and open to receive any messages you are to receive. In the animal kingdom, these senses are enhanced for them, they are detached from the emotions, comforts and needs that humans have. They so easily tap into these senses and utilize them to increase their survival and quality of life— in turn we are doing the same thing. While animals may not be conscious beings, they are still ones that are able to remain with high tastes of taste, touch, smell, hear, feel, see and know. If they loose sight of any of these things, they risk the chance of disease or death. The increased sense you experience will connect you back with the natural world, the instinctual self.

One of the most important lessons about this phase, is not only realizing that you have these senses and abilities, but that they are innate and God given, meaning you don't have to do anything but nurture your natural abilities and intelligence, not to be above, but to actually experience homeostasis– a place where you are acclimated, self-aware, physically and mentally healthy. Its good to remember that each of us need these parts of ourselves to be in tune with the larger parts of life. While its not particularly "special" it is a blessing to know we are poised to have our senses no matter how involved we get with them. All of these will give new meaning to the phrase "senseless action" because you'll know without a doubt that the reference is about not being aware, not thinking or sensing clearly.

Psychic Abilities

Psychic abilities are nothing more than a heightened awareness of our senses. However with a psychic you may possess abilities the regular senses may not pick up on. Some people are able to see premonitions with their psychic abilities– seeing an event before its manifested in physical form. You can likely feel or hear things before other's can, or can sense tones that are low frequency and undetectable by others. There is another spin off that includes seeing people from other realms that have passed on, which is called being a Medium. Whatever the capability you find yourself being aware that you have, realize this is a process of awakening to yourself and not an episode of psychosis— do your best to keep this approach logical.

There is one way to compartmentalize all of the different ways you experience increased Psychic abilities and that is to enhance and focus on the clairsenses.

The Clairsenses

The word "clair" is from the french word clear and brings the full meaning of the word to be "clear senses". They are our natural gifts and working on the self can help develop a more heightened awareness around what we see and sense. It is the survival instinct that looks for protection by giving a person more awareness, to help a person develop skill around the decisions that are made. The concept is that you are able to make a more informed decision about if you have enough "information" about it. The clairsenses are an intelligent system designed to give extra perceptions of the world, its made up of intricate control centers that give heightened states of intuitive understanding and inner knowledge. This is where psychic ability can be logically understood and where you might be able to deduce the special ways you sense things around you. Hone in on the ones you feel exceptional at until the rest begin to develop. Remember that not all people develop each one to extreme levels, what may occur is more emphasis on one or a few.

Clairvoyance-Seeing
This is our sight, quite literally what we see in front of us, although that perception may vary from person to person. It is the ability to see past what the two eyes view and often calls upon the third eye to enhance this feature. It allows one to realize they have the ability to look into the past, present, or future. Clairvoyance can also look like recalling something that feels true and oftentimes ends up being so. People have reported increased awareness around clairvoyance when they see things others cannot and pick up on images that cannot be seen with the naked or untrained eye.

Other examples of this sense being deeply activated are sparks of light or seeing things in your peripheral view. They could be intense, enlightening dreams that predict an event or prompt you to call and ask someone if they are okay because an image of their face graced your minds eye. Also the inclusion of seeing spirits, angels, or the resemblance of people that have passed on, like our beloved family members. Some see auras, shadows, and silhouettes of people they do not recognize.

One way to work with this skill is to begin taking less focus off of particular objects in nature and to use the eyes to scan the whole landscape. This allows you to open your view and allow more to come into sight. This activity is best used while looking out the window and not performing any tasks such as driving. You may not notice anything striking about what you are looking at, but the object is to open your sight to encompass all "points of view" instead of having one focal point.

Clairaudience- Hearing
This is what we can directly and indirectly hear. This can range from any of the normal sounds of the day to day like traffic, neighboring pets, and people moving around to very low tones and frequencies that sound like a whisper. It can mean literal voices outside of yourself or more commonly the voices inside your head– who you think as yourself. Do you listen to yourself when something inside you says to go the other way, visit the store down the road, or hold off on that purchase? This is closely tied to intuition, but could be understood as actually hearing another voice tell you what you should do based on a feeling– following your gut instinct. Clairaudience can be coupled with clairsentience because they can both piggy back off each other by using feeling as the determining factor to "hear" what the right choice is.

The reality however is that hearing encompasses more than just an audible sound, it encompasses a higher frequency, picking up the small nuances of sound waves. This is best described as having an encounter with someone and as soon as you hear their voice you are automatically alert, in tune and engaged. They emit a radio wave that is of a higher vibration and you can intrinsically feel how good it actually is, therefore it makes you feel like you've known the person forever, or they like you, have the ability to discuss subjects that are of high calabur for long periods of time.

Its hearing encouraging words and taking it into the body, resulting in goose bumps, feelings of elation, or feeling overcome with emotion. This also includes the hearing impaired community as they feel and respond to vibrations and sound currents through their body— hearing is not just done with the ears. Hearing is an all encompassing experience— you utilize your other senses to get you to higher frequencies and vibrations. These vibrations not only keep you on higher ground and level mind, but you are more apt to be open to experiences that enrich your life and staying away from ones that don't.

Clairsentience- Feeling
The part of us the senses our body and its reaction to what we are experiencing in life. Its here where we realize if something feels good or not and what

will prompt us to stay away. We can solely base our decisions on the way we feel and use our gut as the leader to making choices, often thinking its our mental ability that is driving our decision. By now you are starting to realize how each sense is helping the other adjust and calibrate so you are able to freely move through life. When we open up to the Kundalini and all it has to offer, we start to feel more in the body, especially if we are utilizing our yoga practice. You become aware of where the feelings are coming from, what events sparked the feeling and how to adjust yourself to feel better. It's a matter of being in your body and picking up the nuance and subtle feelings in every limb to the tip of the nose. Feeling your way to reasoning and coming to a logical conclusion.

It then develops into feeling energy outside of yourself that may not belong to you. Possessing the ability to go into a room and feel the energy of everyone around you, knowing who to stay away from and wether you should stay or go. You'll begin to detect when you should take care of certain tasks, tracking if there is a pattern, or the ability to sense if the feeling is new. Clairsentience can awaken old feelings, like you are presently in that moment once again or catapult you into future feelings. It purely depends on your personal experience with it as some paths include more extreme realities such as actually feeling entities or spirits— which can feel like a gift for some.

Claircognizance- Knowing
The experience of knowing is a mental, emotional, and physical process that utilizes clairsentience, clairaudience, and clairvoyance to make it come to life. It's the feeling of being absolutely sure about something mentally and willing to move forward. But in fact, its larger than that and encompasses what we've covered in the book up until now, and that is having a trust in the bigger picture. Knowing life has to offer far more than you could possibly conjure for yourself. When you believe in something higher than yourself, and put trust and faith into that process, you find yourself with claircongnizance– to be led by more.

Ultimately this is the way of intuition and being led by an internal calling. Some recognize this as a bold move to quit their job only to find out that three months after they left, the company went bankrupt or selling a home before the market crash. People can find themselves jumping the gun on situations only to realize it was the best choice they could have made. They listened to their inner guidance regardless of what they thought could happen, feeling the risk and knowing you'll be protected no matter how you land. People that hone in on this sense are able to take extreme risks that others may not and come out on the other end unscathed, however there are cases in which the outcome isn't as positive as everyone would hope. In any case, the freedom to choose, take risk, and look outside yourself for inspiring ways to move in the world is what claircognizance brings to a persons life.

How To Integrate The New You

The way we integrate these experiences we find ourselves in is to take a moment and reflect how it actually feels for you. Rather than being told how to feel, this book is to keep you informed so you control what process to follow and what you'd like to absorb. The importance above all to understand at a core level that you do not need to encompass everything mentioned in this book. It takes time to allow everything to move around in your life, so that you have access to these experiences as the years progress.

While this process is an eye opening and enlightening one, it is best practice to stay humble on your journey so you remain open in your energy centers and open to the opportunities that will come your way. As you start relating more to your senses, raising your vibration and utilizing your practices, something starts to occur that is undeniably profound. You realize life starts to speed up on you as in, you may loose track of time throughout your day, forgetting the days of the week and months as a lot starts to meld together. This occurs primarily because when you start to grow in this area of your life, you run through experiences, lessons, and iderations very quickly. You can make a decision to move somewhere and within a week you have secured the place and have been contacted out of the blue for a job. You can find yourself wanting to be a part of a program, getting in only to realize you made it just in time, registration closed the day after you signed up. As you jump from place to place it seems as if people were waiting for you to arrive, only to close the doors as soon as you do. You're speeding up, to catch up to the greater parts of your life experience.

You may find yourself detaching yourself from your watch as you get lost in the activities you choose to spend your time on and those activities get larger as the months and years pass by. You start to become the person you always envisioned with a purpose and drive for life. The goals and hopes for life become less lofty and begin to materialize without much work on you part, events or opportunities making you feel as you hadn't asked for it, but internally, it was what you wanted.

Integrating the new you is more about what you allow and less of what you actually control. You'll come to quickly realize that if you resist or give hard definitions around plans, you will be sorely surprised that it doesn't turn out in your favor. While not being able to plan or control every aspect of your life and inner awakening, you realize rewarding the process of letting go can actually be.

Restricting the use of debilitating words opens up the floodgates of what could occur for your life experience. If there are no hard lines to how it needs to turn up, can it then come how it wants? What if the specificity left out all of the beautiful things you didn't know could be a part of the experience? You might realize a lot of what comes into your life that brings the greatest amounts of joy aren't exactly what we asked for or anticipated—spontaneity ushers in synchronicity and unexpected events to occur.

Remembering that your journey is unique to you is the catalyst for being a part of groups where people like you, are following this way of life. While the particulars about what each of you experience is vastly different, there is support and understanding that can shine a positive and supportive light. Too often times we suffer by ourselves with thoughts and feelings that cant be explained away by our own logic. It can be scary to be in this state of mind and not knowing who to talk to if something feels off. This is why its important to remember that partners, family members, and children should be handled with care if they are not on this journey with you. They do not know what to expect or what you are going through. Explaining the initial process of wanting to ask yourself deeper questions about life, the memories and painful traumas that may resurface from time to time should be kept for those who understand how to receive you.

As you become stronger in your approach by getting intimate with your practice and your understanding of what it means to live in a conscious way you'll begin to notice your autonomy increase. Not having to rely on anyone to get the things you need is imperative. The ability to stand alone and hold yourself upright through challenges shows as resiliency and quickly you'll realize how resourceful you have become. Trusting yourself can give you so much freedom from needing others, yet can bring you so close because you are able to contribute your strength— interdependence, a true virtue. So the idea is to yes, be an independent, free thinking person as you've always been, but this is what you contribute to the whole of your groups and people you interact with, thus creating more like minded people who give what they've got.

CHAPTER ELEVEN
Conclusion & Aftercare

As you wind down to the last few objectives of this book, I hope you have come to realize just how special this journey is not only for your happiness and well being, but for the collective and our ability to attain the same heights as you— if one person can do it, the possibility is open for everyone to walk this way of life.

So often in life we are probed to make changes in our lives without the support to back it up. Far too often we are left without directives on how to navigate life's tricky lessons and road blocks or to even be received in a nurturing way, considering all avenues to continue arduously on target. Here we hope to insert a little TLC and remind you how much your health and well being means so this process is successful— your progression is our progression.

Good Practices To Follow When Doing Spiritual Work

Here we will discus the importance of knowing where you stand on your journey so you are set up for success. Being a beginner can be difficult because there is so much information out there about the subject of spiritual matters and awakening the Kundalini, but one of the best practices when starting out is limiting the amount of different information you consume– be selective. The reason for this extends past taking information from people who are not actually spiritually inclined, but possibly being ushered to do something you are not ready for. As you continue walking along the path of self-knowledge you will thirst for more as you touch all the pieces that peak your interests. When you feel ready and had the chance to try all the practices in this book, then consuming more about each subject is recommended and encouraged. There is far more information about the topics of Yoga, Meditation, awakening the Kundalini, and opening the third eye. Each subject circulates around ancient practices that have been recorded and ritualized for thousands of years.

Becoming a student of life is a great way to stay on top of the latest research on these topics and for you to analyze and draw conclusions about your own experience as you do more research by reading books, watching documentaries, and take measures to be a part of groups who also participate and walk this life.

Recommendations For Staying Mentally Healthy

Staying mentally healthy is a goal all of us want to achieve wether we are doing spiritual work or not. More often than not we are left to our own devices allowing our minds to run the show, where the mind goes the body follows and that can be a recipe for disaster– the body and mind must be a unit that functions together or you remain disconnected to your experience and expansion. When you are mentally healthy you are emotionally fit, meaning you are prepared to take on situations with a level head and strong handed approach. The practices outlined in this book not only get you to the awakening, but also keep you even keep and mentally level.

Meditation, while not the easiest task to pick up, can be the easiest once practiced just 2 times, the body starts to notice what It can do when you take time out of your day to not focus and just "be". What's not widely known is the easiest way to get to a meditative state is to be active first, this is why Yogic practices or restorative body movements perpetuate a meditative state after the body has experienced its rushes of adrenaline and dopamine. When you feel exhausted from moving the muscles, aligning the body properly and taking part in rigorous breathing, the body comes to a state of homeostasis— a place where the body is neutral, satisfied and responsive.

With over 50 meditations, affirmations, and yogic breathing techniques provided in this book, you could easily practice one a week for the rest of the year and have a full and complete understanding of each. Each one gives you the opportunity to see if the specific meditation or exercise works for you. Taking a week for each one allows you to develop a practice on your own terms and get creative with the way you'd like to approach it. If you approach it seriously, there is no right or wrong way to approach it and you are encouraged to take the path into your own hands.

Using Meditation

Using Meditation to clear the mind and calm down the nervous system is imperative for healthy bodily function, not to mention, putting your mind at ease. When utilizing the meditation practices provided in this book as well as your own self discovery with Mindfulness meditation you will start to notice something different around the way you perceive your day and daily experiences. Just a few moments a day can allow you to drop into peace and let go of a few words or thoughts that wouldn't be self serving if they were kept. You don't need to become the best meditator in the world, nor do you need to do it for hours a day to enjoy the benefits, you only need to sit for a few moments, 5 at minimum to start and increase the time as you feel more comfortable. In no time, you'll be sitting for 20 minuets or more a day because its feels good.

After time, sinking into meditation becomes a place of nostalgia and you'll learn to appreciate what the inner side of your eyelids look like on a daily basis, as it truly becomes a place of home. It's yet another way your body can reach consistent levels of homeostasis and increased feelings of ease and well being. Meditation can become something you practice in your car before, during or after work, it can be what you do on your lunch break or what you do right after taking a shower. You get to utilize this practice the way you see fit and the more you can associate the practice with what your daily routine, the easier it will be to maintain the practice to develop higher states of consciousness.

Using Visualization To Manifest Your Future Desires

Using visualization to manifest what you hope to see for your future is one way we can take the practice of prayer and use it to our advantage without the tinge of religion or doctrine. Many people tout this as the next new thing to practice in order to get the material possessions you want in life and while that idea is close, its not always the full story. What you can actually manifest, is what's for your highest and greatest good and that doesn't always equate to getting exactly what you want, but rather what you need. On the contrary, It can bring to your life things you didn't ask for, cataclysm you weren't expecting and a chain of events that remove things from your life– not add more.

When using visualization, its best not to control the narrative when you visualize, instead allow your consciousness to open up and show you what the inner parts of you desires. When you are open to anything happening, you get to your results a lot quicker. For example, if you have an idea fixed in your head that you want to be a millionaire and you seek to visualize the exact things you want to buy and where you'd like to live specifically, you eliminate all other forms this could come as. If instead you visualize wealth, helping others and focusing on the feelings of not worrying about money, it can manifest how its supposed to. Who says billionaire isn't an opportunity– go general instead of specific.

So yes, ask for the experiences you'd like to have, just don't have the whole road mapped out in your mind from beginning to end, that way you invite more possibilities of the outcome. It is sure to provide a far larger experience than your imagination could have come up with. Trust the process in visualization and give it a try, many of them located in the meditation section of this book and you are encouraged to feel comfortable enough to take a visualization on your own, guided by only your thought processes.

Music: Keeping Your Vibration High With Harmony

Music is one of the most important essences in our hearing experience because the tones, harmonies and melodies provide a person with a sense of harmony, balance, and peace depending on what it is you're listening to. Take notice to any songs with words, do these words resonate with the person you are today? And if they are not, why do you continue to sing them? Does the beat of the song bring you to states of joy and happiness, or move you to tears because you feel joy, sorrow, or sadness? If you get no emotional response, why do you listen?

It's a conscious thought about what we take in and allow to permeate our being. You may notice songs without words elicit different emotional responses, music where the language is not known to you, or listening to mantra's from yogis. Diversify what you listen to and connect personally so you can attain the higher frequencies of what music truly offers—elation, joy, and a grateful approach to being alive.

Remember that when you listen to music you take on the energy of the song, the artist and the vibrations emitted.

Conclusion & Where To Go From Here

There are many different roads you can find yourself on after going through the concepts in this book. You can put it down, walk away, and never think about it's contents again, which doesn't seem likely, or you can take what you've learned and apply as much of it as feels good to you. Or you can also get very deeply spiritual as you see the connections and realize there is more to life you'd like to play with.

Firstly, remove all expectations of perfection and what it looks like to walk on this path– remember that we all look different while doing it. We see a lot of images these days with social media and the ideas of what spiritual looks like is definitely not it. The longer you're in the game, the easier it will be to spot these images for any true authenticity, through your own experience you'll realize how hard it is to actually look like the images you see. Its not fancy clothes, vast amounts of gemstones, or white clothes. Its your own raw process of it all and stylistically its all your own.

Secondly, remain open about the journey and what you find yourself faced with. When life is approached from a standpoint that "everything happens for a reason, I just don't see it yet", then you might find yourself at ease more often than not when things occur that you didn't anticipate.

Lastly, you should be extremely proud that you desire and are trying to attempt to expand your consciousness through awakening the Kundalini and opening the third eye. Following the practices outlined not only gives you a leg up by knowing parts of the process to expect, but gives you the ultimate freedom to do with it what you want and create routines that fit who you are and how you live your life day to day.

Life will only get more expansive from here, may you be safe on your journey, may you be loved completely, and may you find what you seek.

SECTION 4: GUIDED MEDITATIONS FOR YOUR PATH

MEDITATION FOR PROTECTION
begin with this meditation anytime you are working with heavy energy or feel like you need something before you start your day

Please close your eyes and take a few deep breaths while you visualize a lighthouse at the shore of a rocky ocean coast. As you hear the waves crash you look up to watch the light go around the top of the lighthouse, over and over its mesmerizing, and soon you find yourself hypnotized by the circular movement– light shining in every direction. As this light goes round and round repeat to yourself " I am protected, I am light, I am love", " I am protected, I am light, I am love"," I am protected, I am light, I am love". Redirect your concentration from the light as you close your eyes. Take a deep breath in, hold for 5 counts and exhale. Again. Take a deep breath in and imagine a safe home and safe travel, hold for 5 counts and exhale. One last time, take a deep breath in and recall why you have a strong and safe foundation, hold for 5 counts and exhale slowly while you sit relaxed, unfazed, refreshed and protected.

MINDFULNESS MEDITATION
Start with this meditation anytime you wanting to practice mindfulness meditation and can be done for any length of time, start with 3 minuets and increase to your level of comfort

In a comfortable seated position you will just relax and try to remove yourself from the thoughts of needing to meditate. Stop thinking about what you forgot, or what you should go get to make sure this process goes well and smoothly, it will, don't worry. Take a deep breath in and gently let the breath out. You may notice sounds around you, buses, ambulances, cats, or your neighbors, as you notice these sounds, you can take another deep breath in and gently allow the air to leave your body. Inhale and exhale. Notice your breath as you breathe in and slowly exhale. You may start to feel sensations in the body, its okay. Breathe in and gently exhale. Breathe in and gently exhale. Breathe in and gently exhale. As thoughts come into your awareness, observe them, but don't let the thoughts change where you are right now. Breathe in and gently exhale. Breathe in and gently exhale. When you are complete you may blink your eyes open and savor your day.

MEDITATION FOR CLEARING THE FIRST CHAKRA: HEALING THE ROOT
In a comfortable seated position, straighten your back by arching it slightly and lifting your chest high,

roll your neck to get some flexibility in the shoulders. Be sure your sit bones are firmly planted, don't be afraid to move and lift the flesh around your thighs to make sure you feel firmly planted. Place the backs of your hands on the tops of your thighs, palms to the sky as you put your hands in Gian Mudra. First finger and thumb will touch at the tips making a zero while the other fingers stick out straight in front of them, stacked together. Take three long deep breaths, each one bringing you deeper into your body, each one relieving tension in the chest and back. Check your posture again, back straight, chest up, and chin slightly tucked in.

Bring your awareness to the area that is making contact with the ground, this is your root, the place where you create and join with another and the place where you eliminate. As you bring your awareness to this area, notice if you feel any sensations in this area, pulsing, tingling, or if there is no sensation at all, that's okay too. Continue to relax as you visualize the color red while still having full awareness of this area. If anything comes to your mind, observe it, but do not allow it to change your emotions just yet, continue to breathe and visualize red. We call upon our higher being for healing the root of our body and keeping us protected. May the lessons of this journey come forth in love and in time. Inhale long deep breaths and exhale the air completely from your lungs.

Place your hands on your knees and begin to move your upper body (Navel up) in a circular motion, using your hands as leverage and only going as big as your body will allow. Inhale and exhale completely as you move your body in 7 slow and steady rotations. When complete, inhale deeply and exhale with an open mouth three times. You may sit here as long as you need, you did an amazing job.

FIRST CHAKRA SELF CARE & HEALING PRACTICES
Be sure to drink plenty of water and only practice this meditation in a safe environment. Caring for this chakra involves keeping the digestive system healthy so elimination can occur more easily. Taking time to eliminate completely is extremely important. Focus on the material you cover this area with and lean on the side of natural fabrics and cotton that can allow air to flow in. Taking long baths with no additives and the use of enemas can greatly improve the healing in the Root Chakra.

MEDITATION FOR CLEARING THE SECOND CHAKRA: HEALING THE SACRAL
In a comfortable seated position, straighten your back by arching it slightly and lifting your chest high, roll your neck to get some flexibility in the shoulders. Be sure your sit bones are firmly planted, don't be afraid to move and lift the flesh around your thighs to make sure you feel firmly planted. Place the backs of your hands on the tops of your

thighs, palms to the sky as you put your hands in Gian Mudra. First finger and thumb will touch at the tips making a zero while the other fingers stick out straight in front of them, stacked together. Take three long deep breaths, each one bringing you deeper into your body, each one relieving tension in the chest and back. Check your posture again, back straight, chest up, and chin slightly tucked in.

Bring your awareness to the area of your body that contains your reproductive organs– the base of the spine and all organs around it. Allow your mind to focus on this area while visualizing the color orange. Allow anything to come up for you that may need your mental attention, if you find yourself in an emotional place, let it out. Notice if this area has any sensations that you can feel and observe if they are linked with a specific state or emotion. We call upon our higher self for healing the reproductive organs and base of our spine, may we stay protected in this process. May the lessons of this journey come forth in curiosity and be free from judgment. Inhale long deep breaths and exhale the air completely from your lungs.

Sit in a comfortable upright position, legs crossed and bring your arms up over your head, gently sweep them parallel to the ground as you bend at the hip and extend your left arm up and over your head, creating an elongated stretch across your legs. Stretch your arm as far left as it will go and then bring yourself back to center. Again you will bring arms to a parallel stance, bend at the hip and stretch the right arm over the head as you bend your body to the side feeling the stretch from the hand all the way down to the hip. Repeat this as many times as it feels right to you. When complete, inhale deeply and exhale with an open mouth three times. You may sit here as long as you need, you should be proud of yourself.

SECOND CHAKRA SELF CARE & HEALING PRACTICES

Be sure to drink plenty of water and continue to work on digestion health and proper elimination. Females benefit from drinking raspberry leaf tea as it promotes reproductive organ and vaginal health. Considering eating earlier in the day so your body has time to digest would be of benefit. Now is the time you should start tracking your water intake so things continue to flush out properly as they heal.

MEDITATION FOR CLEARING THE THIRD CHAKRA: HEALING THE NAVAL

In a comfortable seated position, straighten your back by arching it slightly and lifting your chest high, roll your neck to get some flexibility in the shoulders. Be sure your sit bones are firmly planted, don't be afraid to move and lift the flesh around your thighs to make sure you feel firmly planted. Place the backs of your hands on the tops of your thighs, palms to the sky as you put your hands in

Gian Mudra. First finger and thumb will touch at the tips making a zero while the other fingers stick out straight in front of them, stacked together. Take three long deep breaths, each one bringing you deeper into your body, each one relieving tension in the chest and back. Check your posture again, back straight, chest up, and chin slightly tucked in.

Bring your awareness to your navel (belly button) as you remember this was the connection to your mother, your lifeline that carried you to birth. As you focus on this area, visualize the color yellow as you allow creativity to blossom in your mind. We call upon the higher center of our being for healing the navel and bringing forth the drive and intensity to live life on purpose. Inhale long deep breaths and exhale the air completely from your lungs.

As you continue your seated posture, back straight, chest up and chin slightly in, you will breathe in and out rapidly through the nose as your belly rises and falls with each inhale and exhale. Inhale and the belly is expanded, exhale and the navel is pushed in toward the spine. Go at your own pace, but focus on steady inhalation and exhalation as you gently move your belly in and out. Don't worry, with time this will get easier. When you've had enough take a deep breath in, hold the breath, 3, 2, 1, and exhale, releasing old stale energy. Take another deep breath of creativity, hold the breath, 3, 2, 1, and exhale out the things people may think of you.

THIRD CHAKRA SELF CARE & HEALING PRACTICES

Practice this breathing exercise– fire breath– starting with 2 minuets and working your way up to 10. This exercise helps strengthen the core, stimulates digestion, and ushers in new Prana for creative self expression. Keep belts and tight fitting clothing around the belly to a minimum. Mindfulness around eating and fullness of the belly needs to be monitored– if we eat too much or too late in the day, digestion cannot happen properly, thus creating blockages our chakra system.

MEDITATION FOR CLEARING THE FOURTH CHAKRA: HEALING THE HEART

In a comfortable seated position, straighten your back by arching it slightly and lifting your chest high, roll your neck to get some flexibility in the shoulders. Be sure your sit bones are firmly planted, don't be afraid to move and lift the flesh around your thighs to make sure you feel firmly planted. Place the backs of your hands on the tops of your thighs, palms to the sky as you put your hands in Gian Mudra. First finger and thumb will touch at the tips making a zero while the other fingers stick out straight in front of them, stacked together. Take three long deep breaths, each one bringing you deeper into your body, each one relieving tension in the chest and back. Check your posture again, back straight, chest up, and chin slightly tucked in.

Bring your awareness to the center of your chest, focusing on your heartbeat. Visualize the color green as you imagine the heart pumping blood to all of your organs and emotionally opening up to bigger and brighter expressions. Place your hands over your heart,"calling upon the higher center of the body for grounded, diplomatic grace. There is an ask to for the heart to remain safely open and to continue to be a beacon for the right interaction in life". Take a deep loving breath in by expanding the chest as far as it will go, hold the breath, 3, 2, 1, and exhale, releasing heartache. Take another deep breath of compassion, hold the breath, 3, 2, 1, and exhale out negativity.

As you continue your seated posture, back straight, chest up and chin slightly in, you will breathe in and out regularly as you make your hands into fists and gently thump your chest. Speed up the process once you get the hang of the feeling, beating slightly harder, but not enough to hurt yourself. Do this for one minute and then relax. Sit still as you witness the sensation you created, feel the energy used to wake the heart and keep it open.

FOURTH CHAKRA SELF CARE & HEALING PRACTICES

Emotions may need additional support from loved ones or trained professionals. Hibiscus tea helps regulate one's blood pressure, recommended to consume during heart opening and times of high stress to support the heart. Reducing caffeine intake will help with the regulation of the adrenal and circulatory systems.

MEDITATION FOR CLEARING THE FIFTH CHAKRA: HEALING THE THROAT

In a comfortable seated position, straighten your back by arching it slightly and lifting your chest high, roll your neck to get some flexibility in the shoulders. Be sure your sit bones are firmly planted, don't be afraid to move and lift the flesh around your thighs to make sure you feel firmly planted. Place the backs of your hands on the tops of your thighs, palms to the sky as you put your hands in Gian Mudra. First finger and thumb will touch at the tips making a zero while the other fingers stick out straight in front of them, stacked together. Take three long deep breaths, each one bringing you deeper into your body, each one relieving tension in the chest and back. Check your posture again, back straight, chest up, and chin slightly tucked in.

Bring your awareness to your throat and all the organs between your ears and shoulders. While you focus on this area of your body, visualize the color blue as it cools these area's of your body. Allow emotions about communication and not being heard come to the surface if needed. Calling upon self directed knowledge to assist in healing the throat will bring words of wisdom and the patience to remain silent so others voices can be heard.

"Let's now ask the throat to speak how we truly feel inside and to use the voice when its most needed". Take a deep cool breath in, hold the breath, 3, 2, 1, and exhale, releasing untold stories. Take another deep breath of self confidence, hold the breath, 3, 2, 1, and exhale speculation.

As you continue your seated posture, back straight, chest up and chin slightly in, you will chant the word Om (oh-m) and repeat it in a tone that feels comfortable. You want to feel the vibration in the wholeness of your head and heart. Repeat this mantra until you begin to feel the blissful or moved by your actions.

FIFTH CHAKRA SELF CARE & HEALING PRACTICES

Practice this mantra starting with 1 minuet and working your way up to 5. Drinking plenty of lemon water is important as the vocal cords begin to heal and be sure to cover your neck during periods of working wit the throat chakra. You may cover your neck with a scarf or clothing that covers the neck and chest fully. Stock up on natural throat lozenges and drink Mullein tea if you find yourself needing to clear out the lungs to continue your mantra.

MEDITATION FOR CLEARING THE SIXTH CHAKRA: HEALING THE THIRD EYE

In a comfortable seated position, straighten your back by arching it slightly and lifting your chest high, roll your neck to get some flexibility in the shoulders. Be sure your sit bones are firmly planted, don't be afraid to move and lift the flesh around your thighs to make sure you feel firmly planted. Place the backs of your hands on the tops of your thighs, palms to the sky as you put your hands in Gian Mudra. First finger and thumb will touch at the tips making a zero while the other fingers stick out straight in front of them, stacked together. Take three long deep breaths, each one bringing you deeper into your body, each one relieving tension in the chest and back. Check your posture again, back straight, chest up, and chin slightly tucked in.

Bring your awareness to the middle of your forehead, but slightly slower– the brow line. Keep your eyes closed as you turn you two eyes up to look at the brow. (If the eyes were open, you'd be cross eyed) Keep your closed eyes focused up as you visualize the color Indigo (deep royal blue) as you allow the strength of the eyes to create a new gaze. If you find your eyes get tired quickly, relax them and resume when you are ready, with time you'll be able to hold the posture longer. " Let's call upon the higher center of the mind to bring the foresight and internal sight needed to continue the path of self-knowledge". Take a refreshing breath in, hold the breath, 3, 2, 1, and exhale, releasing missed opportunity. Take another deep breath of trust, hold the breath, 3, 2, 1, and release self doubt.

SIXTH CHAKRA SELF CARE & HEALING PRACTICES

Practice this eye posture starting with 1 minuet and working your way up to 5. This exercise helps strengthen the eyes and increase functional capacity within the eye. Be sure to protect your eyes from the sun. Reducing the amount of negative influence you observe will be of great benefit. Peppermint tea may soothe any headaches that occur when working with this area. Improving your sleeping area and increasing the amount of quality sleep you receive will be paramount.

MEDITATION FOR CLEARING THE SEVENTH CHAKRA: HEALING THE CROWN

In a comfortable seated position, straighten your back by arching it slightly and lifting your chest high, roll your neck to get some flexibility in the shoulders. Be sure your sit bones are firmly planted, don't be afraid to move and lift the flesh around your thighs to make sure you feel firmly planted. Place the backs of your hands on the tops of your thighs, palms to the sky as you put your hands in Gian Mudra. First finger and thumb will touch at the tips making a zero while the other fingers stick out straight in front of them, stacked together. Take three long deep breaths, each one bringing you deeper into your body, each one relieving tension in the chest and back. Check your posture again, back straight, chest up, and chin slightly tucked in.

Bring your awareness to the top of your head, the area we never see, but it exposed to so much in life. As you focus your energy, visualize the color purple emanating from the top of your head like a lighthouse. "There is a call to he heavens for healing the crown and allowing the messages above to imprint the fabric of our life". Take a cosmic breath in, hold the breath, 7,6,5,4, 3, 2, 1, and exhale, releasing everything you thought you knew. Take another deep breath of new life, hold the breath, 7, 6, 5, 4, 3, 2, 1, and release expectation.

As you continue your seated posture, back straight, chest up and chin slightly in, you will breathe in and out rapidly through the nose as your belly rises and falls with each inhale. With your left hand on your knee, you will use the right thumb to cover your right nostril. Cover the right nostril and inhale through the left nostril, you will then switch nostrils using the ring finger to cover the left nostril to exhale out of the right nostril. Again you will inhale through the right nostril, switch fingers and use the thumb to close the right nostril and exhale out of the left. You are basically taking turns inhaling and exhaling through each nostril. *Do this cyclical breathing for as long as you like.* When complete, sit in silence to feel the energy you have just created and cleared from your life.

SEVENTH CHAKRA SELF CARE & HEALING PRACTICES

Keeping the head covered as you practice this meditation will assist in protecting the energy at the top of the head. You may over time find yourself wanting to cover your head and this is a normal process with spiritual practice as many wear turbans, hats, and scarfs while in devotional practice or just moving about their day to protect the energy of the head and aura of the body. Working with this part of the body may increase awareness and understanding of the dream state. Recording what you experience and ideas that come to you greatly benefit the flow of energy. Meditation exercises will increase as the crown gets nurtured and supported with attention and protection.

MEDITATION ON VISUALIZATION
Take a deep breath in, hold for 5 seconds, and exhale. Visualize yourself perched on top of a small grassy hill. The wind is blowing and you can feel the hairs on your head move around rapidly. The smell of sweet flowers graces the wind as it gently blows past your sensitive nose. Catching a butterfly in the near distance you realize you are sitting in a place with the perfect view. Off into the horizon is a span of mountain ranges, valleys, and mesas as far as the eye can reach in a full 360 degree view. Suddenly the sky falls dark and every star in the galaxy creates

pinholes across a black backdrop for you to gaze upon. As you sit in silence and wonderment the sky changes from day to night over and over while you gaze upon cloudless sky's and take the moonlit path of the night. Take a few more moments here to bask in the glory of what you are witnessing in your minds eye. Take a nice long deep breath and bring your awareness back to this present moment, and exhale. Inhale again and hold the breath, 3, 2, 1, and exhale.

MEDITATION ON LEAVING THE PAST BEHIND

Take a safe, quiet, seated position and close your eyes. Imagine the memories you'd like to leave behind as you realize there is a big box to the right of your sight. You go over to it and place the past memories inside the box. Any negative thought patters around the past goes into the box, standing there, you carefully analyze your life and the experiences your mind ruminates on that does not help you progress. As you look down at the box, exhausted from searching, you realize its getting full. Neatly close the box and use the tape beside it to fasten the top shut. Take the box with you to the river you hear down the way. As you stand at the shore with your box full of memories gently place the box in the water and allow the river's current sweep away the memories of the past. Keep your eyes on the box until you are no longer able to see it. Inhale deeply and exhale completely. Inhale again, taking in fresh unburdened energy, and exhale the air out of the lungs completely as you bring your awareness to the present moment.

A MEDITATION FOR CLEARING THE ENERGY OF YOUR HOME

Light an incense, scented candle, or your favorite resin to give burned offering. As you light it repeat "today I cleanse my home with good intention and honest faith, please guide me and my space toward protection". As you walk to each corner of your house, wave your burned offering and repeating "I bless this house, I bless my life" and continue to slowly and intentionally scan your home addressing any corners or areas that feel as if they need refreshment. When you are complete you may allow the rest of the item you chose to burn freely as you open your doors and windows for at least 2 minuets. Allow the cleansing process to finish by ushering the heavy energies out of your space.

*Cleansing any dishes, dumping trash and putting away misplaced items will increase the free flowing energy to move through your home.

A MEDITATION TO CONNECT YOU TO YOUR DREAM STATE

Please close your eyes and sit in a comfortable seated position before you make your way to bed. This meditation is to help your subconscious mind open before you lay your head down to sleep. As you sit here take long deep breaths in and out. Inhale, exhale, inhale, exhale, bring your eyes to focus at your brow (you will be cross eyed) as you look at the Third Eye. Stay here as you continue to take long inhale's and exhale's. If your eyes start to feel tired, take a break and resume the posture when you feel ready. Inhale fully and exhale completely. Bring your eyes to a restful position as they remain closed. You will now listen to these words and take them into your being, believe them, know them and sink into them. It is your sleep mantra that connects you to the ethereal dream world. "Tonight I ask for the memory of my dreams. Tonight I ask for understanding to what occurs when I am unconscious. May I be blessed every night to explore the depths of who I am through traveling and experiencing the adventures in the corners of my mind. May I always be protected. And so it is". Take a moment to continue your stillness as your cells try to catch up with your requests. If you can remember to ask each night before you fall asleep, you will realize more often than not, your ask will come true.

A MEDITATION FOR YOUR NEW GIFTS

In a comfortable seated position, straighten your back slightly and lift your chest high. Be sure your sit bones are firmly planted. Place the backs of your hands on the tops of your thighs, palms to the sky as you put your hands in Gian Mudra. First finger and thumb will touch at the tips making a zero while the other fingers stick out straight in front of them, stacked together. Take three long deep breaths, each one bringing you deeper into your body, each one relieving tension in the chest and back. Check your posture again, back straight, chest up, and chin slightly tucked in. Inhale deeply and exhale completely.

Bring your awareness to the wholeness of your journey so far. Are there things you've realized about yourself that feel enlightening now? Ruminate on one that brings you to a state of freedom and release. Here is where you'll take a moment to give your attention to states of being that have given you the most education about yourself, what have you learned this far? Feel in your heart as these words reach your ears, "I am grateful to the journey ahead of me and the one that lays behind, I feel changed and enlivened by the way I process my life and I look forward to many more years of discovery". And so it is. You may stay here for as long as you need, being sure to give yourself space to digest what comes up.

A MEDITATION FOR DEVELOPING YOUR NEW PRACTICES

As you sit in a comfortable position anywhere you choose, close your eyes and sink into a nice quiet space. Raise your shoulders up to your ears and drop them back to your sides. Roll your head to stretch your neck a few times to get more settled. Take long deep breaths, try your best to allow thoughts to pass, its okay to have thoughts. Stay here as you continue to take deep inhale, long exhale. Inhale, slowly exhale, focus on the breath. Now begin to visualize yourself doing your practices, one after another, day after day, your consistency shines through. Stay here to continue watching your life improve from the small steps you are taking. Remember to include waking up on time to start them and the benefits of being prepared for your life each day. Ruminate on this. Take a deep breath in of possibility, hold the breath, 3, 2, 1, and exhale, releasing doubt. Take another deep breath of grounded practices, hold the breath, 3, 2, 1, and exhale all of the previous failed attempts.

YOGIC BREATHING TECHNIQUES:
ALTERNATE NOSTRIL BREATHING

Sitting in a comfortable seated position, with your left hand on your knee, you will use the right hand to take the thumb and cover your right nostril. Cover the right nostril and inhale through the left nostril, switch nostrils using the ring finger to cover the left nostril to exhale out of the right nostril. Again you will inhale through the right nostril, switch fingers and use the thumb to close the right nostril and exhale out of the left. You are basically taking turns inhaling and exhaling through each nostril. ** Do this cyclical breathing for 1 minuet.* When complete, sit in silence to feel the energy you have just created.

YOGIC BREATHING TECHNIQUES:
COOLING THE BODY AND SENSES

Sit in a comfortable seated position with the spine upright. The back is straight, the chest is up and the chin is slightly tucked in. You will close your eyes and take a few long deep breaths. Fix your mouth into the shape of the letter O as you inhale cool breaths through the mouth and exhale through the nose— you may close your mouth as you exhale if you wish. Inhale cool breath from open mouth and exhale warm air from the nostrils.

*Do this for 3 minutes and include it in your day anytime you need to cool off from hot temperatures or attitudes. Can be done with eyes open in stressful situations such as driving or before test taking.

BONUS MEDITATIONS & AFFIRMATIONS

A MEDITATION FOR THE NEW YOU

As you stand in front of the mirror, get close and observe the pupils of your eyes. Do you recognize the eyes staring back at you? How have you changed physically? Observe the face you may not look at in this way. Notice every freckle, scar, imperfection, and perfection you see. Take full stock in who you see yourself to be.

Take yourself to a comfortable place and sit in a position that works best for you. As you close your eyes, take 3 cooling and cleansing breaths to center yourself. Visualize the person you saw in the mirror a moment ago, what is this person doing now? Keep visualizing yourself moving through your day to day, does it look different than what you do now? Find yourself fitting into the space you'd like to see yourself in and where you would like to be. Find yourself with freedom, wealth, and knowledge to make better decisions. Place your hands over your heart, "may I continue to see myself and continue grow as a healthy and spiritual being", now place your hands in prayer pose and sit here to ponder for as long as you wish.

A MEDITATION TO OVERFLOW WITH FULLNESS
Fullness of life is all around me, seeing what is in store, the bigger picture of it all. I live for all the moments that are unknown and I am unrestrained through my freedom of choice. Imagine a door at the end of a tunnel covered in plant life, wild flowers, and a sense of untamed wildness– it's a door to new opportunity. As you step through the door you realize there are things you've never seen before and you stop to take a look at the first place you notice. What is that place?

Please close your eyes, take a deep breath in, take it to the bottom of your belly, then fill your lungs.

Hold for as long as you can and release it in peace. YOUR LIFE IS FULL.

A MEDITATION TO SCAN THE BODY
In a quiet space, settle into a comfortable seated position. Straighten your spine straight, and elongate the neck. Place your open palms on your knees and gently wiggle your hips to settle your body into place. Close your eyes, and breath at a slowed but steady pace. Begin by concentrating on the crown of your head. Picture each point on your body as you "scan" from your crown down to the tips of your toes. Take a few moments to notice how your body feels as you pass your attention over each point. When you've completed your scan, sit in silence. Mentally ask your body what it needs, how you can be of service to it. Listen carefully to what you're being told.

A MEDITATION FOR FUTURE PATHS
I look towards the future as I digest what's happened to me in the past. I am a polished, forward thinking, and radiant human being. I am not my experiences, I am the perception of what I believe my journey is. I open a window to clear my energy, take in the fresh air and face toward a new outlook. The horizon looks bright and I feel good that I am not limited by my circumstances.

Please close your eyes, take a deep breath in, fill the bottom of your belly, then fill your lungs. Hold for as long as you can and release it in peace. Keep your eyes closed and envision words on a paper tucked away inside a box. As you open this box you realize the words on the paper say words you've always wanted to see for yourself, what does it say? AND SO IT IS.

A MEDITATION TO RISE TO YOUR LIFE

There are two paths you find yourself looking upon. One of them leads to something you've always wanted, but when it you get it, that's it, you have nothing else to look forward to– your life still remains the same. The other path leads you to a road of unlimited potentiality, you'll just never get the choice. Everything will be spontaneous, forever changing, and unplanned. While hard, you realize life has a lot to offer when you go with the flow. As you align with new parts of yourself and revamp your beliefs. Which path shall you choose, staying the same or change?

A VISUALIZATION

There is a door at the top of a staircase, vibrant emerald green and adorned with running vines of golden ivy. Behind the door lay our deepest fears and worst thoughts about ourselves. Recognize that our shadow side, the parts of ourselves we hide from the world, are integral to our growth, they have a story to tell. It may be too difficult for you to enter. It's ok to linger and gently rub your fingers along the golden leaves, or find some delight in the texture of wood beneath your fingertips. Take time to enjoy the cool feel of the brass doorknob. There is no rush, be gentle with yourself - work your way up to turning the knob and opening the door. Know that it is safe to do so, you are cradled in the arms of Source and you are loved.

Please close your eyes, take a deep breath in, fill the bottom of your belly, then fill your lungs. Hold for as long as you can and release you're breath quietly. Keep your eyes closed and envision what its like to have more than you ever thought you could because you opened fully to what life had in store. Sit here for a moment and feel it deep within you as you take another deep breath. RISE TO YOUR LIFE

A MEDITATION FOR HONESTY

I honor the virtue inside of me as I realize everyone on this earth is inherently good. I am honest with myself because I search for my own internal self knowledge. The more honest I get with myself, the more I understand of others— my compassion comes from within and extends to everything around me.

Please close your eyes, take a deep breath in, fill the bottom of your belly, then fill your lungs. Hold for as long as you can and release it with an open mouth while you exhale a cleansing breath. Keep your eyes closed and envision a bright green light in the center of your chest, watch it emanate past your chest and surround your body creating a bright aura of gorgeous natural green energy. Stay here as you extend this aura 100 feet, keeping this bright glow in your minds eye for as long as possible. Feel it deep within you as you take another deep breath and exhale. HONESTY WITH YOURSELF IS YOUR GIFT THIS LIFETIME.

A MEDITATION FOR RECEIVING TRANSMISSIONS
This is a transmission to guide you in unlocking your intuitive response to your inner most desires. I hold the keys to my success today and everyday, so what does that success look like to me?

As you stay here a wile to contemplate, try your best to understand how you might get to this place. Do you struggle to start because you have fear around attaining an end goal? What do you honestly feel holds you back from what is truly desired?

Please close your eyes as you take a deep inhale. Contemplate about the messages that came to you while keeping compassion in your heart for your very unique process. NEVER STOP LISTENING.

A MEDITATION FOR MY INNER PEACE
My inner peace comes from the quiet spaces I find myself in. Where I feel the comfort of my world through the warmth on my skin, a satisfied belly, and just enough to make it work in my favor. I understand that I control my sense of inner peace

through my practices, connection to my body and achieving brief states of a still and calm mind. No one can take this peace, no one can change this peace, I control my sense of inner peace.

Please close your eyes while you take 3 long deep inhales and exhales. Hold each inhale for as long as you can before exhaling. Imagine a park bench in the middle of a highway, cars rushing by you as your eyes are closed, all you can hear are birds chirping, don't they sound beautiful? YOU CONTROL YOUR SENSE OF INNER PEACE

A MEDITATION TO PREPARE FOR THE LONG ROAD
It's a long road, there is no turning back. Setting sights on the new me, I realize this road is long, winding and forever changing. Once I have begun, I cannot turn back because I continue to evolve and expand who I am through self knowledge. I achieve a lifetimes worth of reward through following a life guided by the road.

Please close your eyes and take 3 cleansing inhales and exhales. Now imagine yourself walking down a road, as you travel you notice it starts to get more beautiful with each step. You didn't quite notice those flowers before and is that fruit you see up ahead? As you continue to walk up the road you feel a sense of comfort as you look behind you to realize you have reached a point where you cant see where you began. IT'S A LONG ROAD, THERE IS NO TURNING BACK.

A MEDITATION FOR DIGNITY

This message is delivered for the support and nourishment of the dignity you hold within you. You are worthy of honor and respect although at times its forgotten. Today you are reminded that you matter, the thoughts you have are valid, and you are worth being treated well and recognized for who you are. Is there someone or some people that have not given you the dignity you so desperately have desired in life? Take a vision of them in your mind, hold it there and tell them "thank you, I love you, and I understand that if you knew better, you would do better". Say that to each person you can think of that has not shown you the respect you hoped for and give yourself the added grace of forgiveness.

Please close your eyes, take a deep breath in, fill the bottom of your belly, then fill your lungs. Hold for as long as you can and release it with an open mouth. Keep your eyes closed while you inhale again giving yourself feelings of love and adoration and exhale again through an open mouth. EASE LIVES HERE

A MEDITATION TO SLOW AND FOCUS ON THE PULSE

Feel the beat of your heart as you slow down your breathing. How does the rhythm feel, is it fast, slow, or steady? Your heart provides a pulse that keeps you alive, you don't have to do anything in order to make it happen, in fact you never have to think about it unless something wrong occurs. Now imagine your heart and what it perceives of your actions and measure of happiness, its working as hard as it can to keep blood pumping through your body to keep you alive.

Now think about all the times you've had to do act in order to make something happen, when you've exerted a lot of effort to get to the goal. Sit here and wander for a bit. What are the achievements you've managed touch– sink in and connect the dots. What are the smells of those memories, were there amazing fruits you tried or foods you ate while brainstorming? Do you remember what it tastes like? What was the weather outside while this focus was taking place? Take a few more moments to allow the rational mind to fade away allowing the memories to come and pass. Deeply ruminate on all of your senses as you release the mental focus on your memories. Take a deep breath in, hold the breath, 3, 2, 1, and exhale, releasing any unwanted feelings. Take another deep breath of love and compassion in, hold the breath, 3, 2, 1, and exhale anything that doesn't serve who you are. I FEEL THE PULSE.

WHO AM I MEDITATION
It is a warm spring day, white fluffy clouds are passing by as you feel a cool and gentle breeze graze

your cheek, you are reminded of something so sweet, what is it? As you take a seat on the grass, you notice how cool and damp it feels and you lean back to prop your hands behind your head and cross your legs. Smile and look up towards the sky, what do you see? As you lay upon the grass sink your shoulders and back into the cold ground making yourself more comfortable. Take a deep breath in and slowly remove your inner self away from your body as you slowly exhale, floating above yourself. Do you see your posture and what you look like? As yourself, ask...who am I?: I SEE WHO I AM

A MEDITATION FOR FRIENDLINESS

In this moment your life is together, your affairs are taken care of, and you are able to rest comfortably—there is nothing you need to do at this moment. As you imagine how easy it is to sit here, imagine yourself leaving to go somewhere like the grocery store and driving to your job. Now that you have some time, you can get to know that person who is always so nice to you, but you never have time to get to know because you're always in a rush. What was their name again? If you could see them now, what would you say to make their day brighter? As you make your way back home there is someone you recognize outside that has a flat tire, are you willing to help them? What was their name again? What would you tell them and would you try to get to know them more? As you now make it into your house, you close the door and smile about the interactions you just had, feeling grateful there are people to connect with. Thank yourself for ushering kindness and compassion to the people you thought about helping and delighted in conversation today. You truly offer value in peoples lives. I AM FRIENDLY AND LOVED

MEDITATION FOR YOUR ANCESTORS

We are honoring the process of our ancestors, remembering what they've brought to our bloodline, the practices they followed and the warmth they shared with us. Today we honor the grandmothers and grandfathers of many generations, thanking them for their contributions to our lineage. Take a deep breath in as you visualize their faces and most positive memories and exhale slowly. The ancestors have paved the way for us to thrive in this lifetime, through their struggles and triumphs, we too share that experience.

Take a deep breath in, hold the breath, 3, 2, 1, and exhale, releasing any unwanted feelings. Take another deep breath of love and compassion in, hold the breath, 3, 2, 1, and exhale anything that doesn't serve who you are. I HONOR MY ANCESTORS.

MEDITATION FOR PASSION

Your passions lie inside of you like an unlit candle, a stone that wasn't overturned, or a seed that hasn't been nurtured yet. Its not something you need to find, its something you need to open your eyes to. Think about who you are in life, how you show up as a friend, partner, coworker, or relative, what do you think they see on the other end and what would you like for them to see about you? When the word passion is mentioned, what is the first thing that comes to mind for you, even if you don't think its something you can achieve or don't know how you will get there, what would it be?

Take a deep breath in as you remember your passion is closely tied to who you show up as each day, hold the breath, 3, 2, 1, and exhale, releasing any unwanted feelings. Take another deep breath in of all your goals and achievements, hold the breath, 3, 2, 1, and exhale uncertainty and doubt about what you think you can do. I AM CONNECTED TO MY PASSION.

A MEDITATION FOR BETTER COMMUNICATION
Communication can bring us to the highest forms of understanding one another and our reality of life. When we spread ourselves out to take in a perception other than our own, we give ourselves the chance to be diverse, active, and the creators of our experiences. Take a deep breath in, hold the breath, 3, 2, 1, and exhale.

Your participation in life makes you a reliable source for communication, a pillar of knowledge, and a master of your domain.

Take a deep breath in, fill the bottom of your belly, then the top of the belly, then lungs and chest. Hold the breath for as long as you can and release it when you feel ready. Keep your eyes closed and bring the conversations you'd like to have to the forefront of your mind. Sit here and ruminate on the discussions, and issues you'd like to resolve. Take another deep breath and exhale through an open mouth. I HAVE BEEN HEARD.

A MEDITATION FOR INTROVERTS
As you sit in a comfortable seated position with the eyes closed, bring the attention to your style of being with people and where you get your energy from. Introverts do like to be around people they trust, but are able to charge the batteries of the soul by taking moments of away to process and where they stand in the world. Whether you identify as an introvert or not, taking moments of solitude can be a way to refresh oneself. Understanding the duality of life means taking in both expressions to appreciate both points of view– to "May you always feel comfortable with who you are and the way you revive your life. Take three long and deep inhale's and exhale's as you release tension from your shoulders and chest. I TRUST MY PROCESS.

A MEDITATION FOR EXTROVERTS

Seated in a comfortable position with the eyes closed, bring your attention to the way you feel when you are out amongst a crowd of people, when you are in groups, or what you seek when you need a pick me up. Focus on the images that come to mind when you think about how pleasurable it is to be with others and to be outside of your immediate environment. Whether you identify as an extrovert or not, some people need the experience of being charged while out with others, in nature or in public places. Inhale deeply, hold the breath, 4, 3, 2, 1, exhale completely and hold the breath out, 4, 3, 2, 1, and inhale. You may relax. I ENJOY THE EXPERIENCES OUTSIDE OF ME.

A MEDITATION TO BE YOUR AUTHENTIC SELF

As you follow your internal guidance system you are being led to give love and pay homage to the person inside, the one who continues to flower as new information comes in to be implemented. If you look back to who you thought you were, what have you learned, and were you close? When you follow along a path in spontaneity, non judgment and expectation, the true authenticity of the self gets a chance to materialize. The more you learn about who you are, the more you notice all other expressions of who you once were fall away. The diligence you apply to your practices get you to deeper aspects of what you truly believe, whether its right or wrong, you are right. Please close your eyes, take a deep breath in, fill the bottom of your belly, then fill your lungs, and exhale gently. Keeping your eyes closed, is there something you'd like to know? Are there messages being transmitted? When you feel ready, take another deep breath, and exhale through an open mouth.

A MEDITATION FOR SELF LOVE

In a comfortable seated position, straighten your back by arching it slightly and lifting your chest high, roll your neck to get some flexibility in the shoulders. Be sure your sit bones are firmly planted, don't be afraid to move and lift the flesh around your thighs to make sure you feel firmly planted. Place the backs of your hands on the tops of your thighs, palms to the sky as you put your hands in Gian Mudra. First finger and thumb will touch at the tips making a zero while the other fingers stick out straight in front of them, stacked together. Take three long deep breaths, each one bringing you deeper into your body, each one relieving tension in the chest and back. Check your posture again, back straight, chest up, and chin slightly tucked in.

Bring your awareness to the center of the chest and focus on the imagery of your heart. Watch your heart as it beats. So many emotions we place here in the chest, the heart deals with the uneven rhythms of our lives and still, without fail, our heart pumps the blood of life into our veins. Take a moment to shower your heart with love and compassion. Take a moment to thank your heart for guiding you to more empowering situations after feeling broken and abused. Thank you heart for the pressure it endures and the relief it provides when we are in love, feel loved, and are giving love. Today the heart will be recognized, as love is poured into its divine process. Today you are recognized as love is poured into your divine process. Love is you, love is all around you, and you are loved.

Bring your awareness to your hands, as they are extensions of the heart. Rub the hands together vigorously using the friction to create heat. Place the heated hands over the heart and repeat, "I am love, love is all around me, and I am loved by others. I am love, love is all around me, and I am loved by others. I am love, love is all around me, and I am loved by others". You may release your hands, take a few cleansing breaths and relax. AND SO IT IS.

AN AFFIRMATION TO INCREASE YOUR SENSE OF ADVENTURE

I am an adventurous person because I am curious about the inner workings of life. I enjoy new experiences because it means there is more to be had. Staying in the same places to repeat the same events and identifying with the experience of other people is not how I feel empowered. I garner strength and self knowledge though knowing that I am not limited by my circumstances and I have the freedom to roam and explore corners of the world

I've never seen. When I awake from sleep, I am happy to be alive, and wonder how far I can get with my goals. When I go to bed at night, I feel grateful for the passing of another day and wish for another to come my way. I live each day for new adventure and I will continue to feed myself with its presence.

AN AFFIRMATION TO REDUCE PAIN

While my body is not perfect, I am conscious enough to help reduce the pain. What I feel is temporary and I possess the knowledge to soothe and bring comfort to what doesn't feel good. I do not identify with pain, only with the ability to feel deeply, to intuit when change is needed, and to know when the body has had enough. I am present enough in my experience to be aware and to intently listen for what needs my attention. I ask my higher self for a break today, to find an avenue to reduce my pain that is healthy and guides me further down my journey of healing. I ask my mind to be easy on me today, to speak to me in ways that nurture instead of beat me down. I ask my body for patience today as I work through the steps to heal the pain it's feeling. I ask that the world be relieved from pain today even if only for a few moments—may we all have the chance to find our grace today. AND SO IT IS.

AN AFFIRMATION FOR HEALING
The path to healing can be marked out with milestones and pitfalls along the way, however they are can be looked at as battle scars, proudly worn with honor. Everyone's journey to healing the self looks the different therefore I choose not to be a victim of my life, but rather a humble hero of my own making. Every obstacle or blessing on my path to self discovery leads me closer to healing. Everyday I heal just a little bit more. Everyday I heal something for someone I love. I ask the higher powers that be to guide me safely through my journey of healing, always pointing me towards the way of soothing my senses, and to connect with those that will guide me to better solutions. AND SO IT IS.

AFFIRMATIONS TO RESHAPE YOUR ROUTINE
When I wake up for the day, I wake up to my life refreshed and ready to start anew. When I wake up to my life I carry none of the worry from the day previous, I move forward, ready and willing. When I move forward with my life new solutions to old problems come my way. When I rise out of bed I give thanks for one more day and one more opportunity to make a difference and effect change in the world. As I move throughout my day, I don't seek perfection, I seek consistency and Im pretty impressed with what I do so far, but I am ready to take on more. I take care to put awareness around the habits I'd like to transform. I enjoy being around

people who allow me to be authentic and seek those relationships more and more each day. I take care to eat well when I am able to, I choose healthy options when they are offered, and I participate in the cooking of my own foods. I take pleasure in the way I provide and prepare nourishment for my body because it prepares me for a good life. When I get home from my day I take care to nourish the living things in my home and put in effort to refresh and prepare my environment for less stress and chaos. As I wind down and lay in bed I look up at the ceiling and catalogue how well my day went, sending blessings to those who need them, while thanking and loving myself for a day well done. I am excited to meet my dreams with openness and take pleasure in knowing another chance to make more out of my life is on the horizon. I love myself, my routine, and work hard to refine my process. I GROW EACH DAY.

A MEDITATION TO HONOR YOUR WATER
This is a meditation to give honor to your water before you consume it. When you take in this water that has been blessed by your kind and loving words of intention and devotion, you take in these words to your body, reaching every cell in your being. Go to your kitchen and pour a glass of water, one you can see through. You can get creative with this by using a pitcher or gallon sized container and fill it will water to have some for later. Sit in a comfortable place with your spine straight and an

open mind. Out loud you will say words of affirmation to your water and over time learn what it is you'd like to say and have permeate through your body. There is no right or wrong way, just practice the concept of loving kindness and your words will lead the way. "I give so much thanks to this cool container filled with nourishment, minerals, and hydration. I love the way you hydrate me, it makes me feel young and alive. I take care not to waste you because I value your impact in my life. Thank you for coming from the earth and thank you for making up 75% of my body. Today I will remember how important it is to honor you". Take a sip of your water and enjoy it as it passes your lips, graces your tongue, hits the back of your throat and eases slowly down the esophagus. Enjoy as you repeat the process knowing all that intention and appreciation is now entering and fulfilling your body.

A MEDITATION TO HONOR YOUR FIRE

Fire is the element of desire, passion, and what we are meant to do with our lives. It manages to ignite something within us that makes our persona and spirit courageous and ready to take on a new challenge, no matter what that is. When you honor your fire, you are honoring your creative process and that is what we intend to do in this meditation. Please come into a comfortable seated position with the spine straight and the eyes closed. Inhale deeply for 3, 2, 1, exhale completely. Inhale as you gather up all your anxieties and exhale all of it out. Visualize a flame on the top of a candle in the center of your belly, at your naval point. Continue to breath deeply as you watch the flame dance around, become still, dim, and then dance again. Focus on size of the flame, can you make it larger? Make the flame as large as you can and let it burn hot. Inhale deeply, exhale completely. As you continue to focus on the flame, allow it to dim once again and finally allow it to go out. Check your posture, back straight, chin back, chest up and out. Inhale deeply, exhale completely as we begin breathing fire. Even breaths through the nose in and out as the belly mimics the nose. Inhale and the belly button is pushed out and exhale the belly button will be toward the spine. As you pump the belly, the air will flow in and out of the nostrils evenly, with time this will be effortless, don't try to hard, just let if flow. Inhale, exhale, inhale, exhale. Listen to the sound of your breath go in and out of your body as you imagine the navel as a hammer pumping against the spine and waking up the creative center– solar plexus. Continue going, don't stop, try not to think just even inhale, exhale, inhale belly is extended, exhale and the belly is contracted and tight. 1 more minuet, you are doing great. INHALE, HOLD, 4, 3, 2, 1, EXHALE. Inhale again and hold, 3, 2, 1, and exhale. REPEAT: I honor my fire, I honor my creativity, I honor my fire, I honor my creativity, I honor my fire, I honor my creativity. Sit here for a moment as Fou behold the energy you have created with the fire in your belly. Remember that this exercise and area of your body is the lifeblood of creative self expression and the chance to create the Prana needed to live long and healthy days. You may relax.

A MEDITATION TO HONOR THE EARTH

When you think of the earth, what comes to mind for you? Is it just the place you live or do you carry more stock into its purpose in your day to day? This meditation is to connect you to the large focus of what the earth is meant to teach us about ourselves. In a comfortable seated position please close your eyes and take a few long and deep cleansing breaths, inhale, exhale, good. Visualize your favorite place to take a walk, notice what draws your attention. The nature is pretty lively today, what animals do you see and what is the mood of the people around you if any? Inhale deeply, exhale completely. As you make your way, what else is particularly noticeable about your walk that you've never noticed before? As you take in the full view and landscape, how is the color? Focus on the colors in your minds eye, allow them to get as vibrant as they can get. Walking along you see a huge patch of bright green, cool, damp, grass. Excited, you kick your shoes off and stand in the grasses glory sinking in the sun as you turn your smiling face to it. Open your hands at your side and allow the rays to hit your palms. Inhale deeply, exhale completely. Now begin to stomp your feet, and clap your hands as no one around you even notices what you are doing, they aren't looking your way as you continue to stomp, clap, smile and enjoy the earth's natural vibrational rhythm working inside you. As you slow your rhythm you come to a seated position on the grass to take in the energy you created and to bask in the suns rays for a little more time. As you sit with your eyes closed and spine straight you take in large, deep, cleansing breaths. Bring your awareness to the fact that you feel grounded at the base of your body, take notice how stable the ground feels beneath you and how good it feels under your feet. Take a few more long deep breaths as you bring your current awareness back to where you sit in the present moment. What are the smells and tastes you have now? Continue to inhale and exhale and when you feel ready you can reWax and open your eyes. Take some time outside today or tomorrow if you can and recreate your dance with the earth.

A MEDITATION INTO THE COSMOS: INNER PLANETS PT. 1

In a comfortable seated position, straighten your back by arching it slightly and lifting your chest high, roll your neck to get some flexibility in the shoulders. Be sure your sit bones are firmly planted, don't be afraid to move and lift the flesh around your thighs to make sure you feel firmly planted. Place the backs of your hands on the tops of your thighs, palms to the sky as you put your hands in

Gian Mudra. First finger and thumb will touch at the tips making a zero while the other fingers stick out straight in front of them, stacked together. Take three long deep breaths, each one bringing you deeper into your body, each one relieving tension in the chest and back. Check your posture again, back straight, chest up, and chin slightly tucked in.

Bring your awareness to the galaxy that conspires above you, the Sun, Moon, Mercury, Mars, Venus, all the personal planets circling around the ecliptic influencing how we feel and what we believe. As above so below, we feel the current of life as it shifts and changes. Imagine the planets circling around you as you sit in silence and peace. Inhale fully, exhale completely. As we narrow the focus we concentrate on the Sun, immediately we feel the warmth this planet gives off as we concentrate on its bright orange/yellow hue. A bright ball of fire starts the day, brings us light, makes food grow, and nourishes all bodies on the planet. The Sun brings with it the determination to begin another day, its what makes us realize we have a purpose and helps us realize what actions we must participate in order to make it happen. Lets take a deep breath in for the Sun and hold the breath, 5, 4, 3, 2, 1, and exhale allowing the belly to soften.

We now take our focus to the Moon, the way we process our life and the personalization we assign to ensure safety, comfort and emotional maturity. If you focus on the color of the Moon you realize the hue is metallic, silver, white, and sparkles if you look at it just right. In our perception depending on the day, we can see the Moon in its various cycles throughout month. From Lunation to Lunation we witness the Moons crescent as it wanes, allowing us to see what lacks and what needs attention. Then we watch the fullness unfold as waxes us to finish what we started, to end and old cycle and prepare for a new one. The Moon is our gracious teacher, giving us a new flavor each day as it makes its way through the Zodiac. Lets take a deep breath in for the Moon and hold the breath, 5, 4, 3, 2, 1, and exhale allowing the legs to soften. Stretch them out and get more comfortable if you feel ready.

Moving on to Mercury, the planet of communication, we realize its not easy to see the color of it, or to even know where it is in the sky if you aren't an avid sky watcher. No matter what, it travels closely to the Sun effecting our lives in the same kinds of cycles as the Moon as it makes its way through the Zodiac. It moves forward and backward through retrogrades, pausing to let us regroup and gather our thoughts before we move on to the next stage. Lets take a deep breath in for the Mercury and hold the breath, 5, 4, 3, 2, 1, and exhale allowing more space in the lungs. REPEAT: "Mercury, please give me the direction to make good choices in where to go and who to talk to", inhale deeply, exhale completely allowing even more room in the lungs.

We will now focus on Mars, the planet of war and our internal determination and motivations. Depending on the time of year, you may be able to see this big red ball of gas in the sky as it flavors our experience making its way through the signs of the Zodiac. Mars can give us determination and the will to stand up for ourselves and what we need to survive. Lets take a deep breath in for the Venus and hold the breath, 5, 4, 3, 2, 1, exhale relaxing all muscles in the face. REPEAT: "Mars, please give me the will to continue the fight and continue to light the path", inhale deeply, exhale completely releasing all tension from the head.

We now venture out to Venus, the planet of love and money. Just as Mercury it may be hard to see the color, but for some inexperienced sky watchers, Venus can still be visible to you. Depending on the time of year and where you are in the world, Venus can show up as a morning star or evening star, either rising before the Sun or setting before the Moon. It's one of the most advantageous planets as it gives us more to strive for. It's the planet that helps us identify what love is and what we need in order to feel satisfied with life. It's the planet that gives us the earning potential needed to gather the resources we are to share with others and save for the future. Lets take a deep breath in for the Venus and hold the breath, 5, 4, 3, 2, 1, exhale allowing more space in the heart. REPEAT: "Venus, please shine through me as I give love and share love, I welcome wealth to come my way", inhale deeply, exhale completely allowing even more room for the heart.

A MEDITATION INTO THE COSMOS: OUTER PLANETS PT. 2

In a comfortable seated position, straighten your back by arching it slightly and lifting your chest high, roll your neck to get some flexibility in the shoulders. Be sure your sit bones are firmly planted, don't be afraid to move and lift the flesh around your thighs to make sure you feel firmly planted. Place the backs of your hands on the tops of your thighs, palms to the sky as you put your hands in Gian Mudra. First finger and thumb will touch at the tips making a zero while the other fingers stick out straight in front of them, stacked together. Take three long deep breaths, each one bringing you deeper into your body, each one relieving tension in the chest and back. Check your posture again, back straight, chest up, and chin slightly tucked in.

Bring your awareness to the galaxy that conspires above you, Saturn, Jupiter, Uranus, and Neptune, all circling around the ecliptic influencing our collective aim. As above so below, we feel the current of life as it shifts and changes. Imagine the planets circling around you as you sit in silence and peace. Inhale fully, exhale completely. As we narrow the focus we concentrate on the Saturn, the planet of time and change. Its what brings you to an understanding that all things come to an end and time moves us on to new experiences. Saturn ushers in the experience of maturation, rising to the higher points of your life so you can deliver your voice, your message, and gifts to society– filling the needs of the time. Lets take a deep breath in for the Saturn and hold the breath, 5, 4, 3, 2, 1, and exhale allowing the whole body to soften. REPEAT: "Saturn, please help me see the path to evolve ", inhale deeply, exhale completely and allow the body to sink deeper.

We will now focus on the actual giant in our solar system, Jupiter. It brings benevolence, higher thinking and makes things larger when next to them. Jupiter gives us a boost of positive motion and helps us have the courage to take risks to understand where extremes lie and where boundaries should be made. Jupiter not only makes things blissful, but gives a slap on the wrist when we are blind to what's in front of us. One of the last planets seen with the naked eye, Jupiter, is always there, pulsing, waiting for the moment to extend its energy to expand and enlarge your perspective, big or small. Jupiter is our benevolent teacher, when we learn all there is to know about reality, we are given new perspectives that help shape and elevate what we have learned–just when you think you know, you realize you have no idea. Lets take a deep breath in for Jupiter and hold the breath, 5, 4, 3, 2, 1, and exhale allowing the thoughts in you mind to soften to soften. REPEAT: "Saturn, please help me see the path to evolve ", inhale deeply, exhale completely and soften the tension around thoughts in your mind.

We will now lend our attention to Uranus, the harbinger of unexpected realties, and one of the last planets to be discovered. Uranus is a gaseous planet that is large and full of surprise as it brings an err energy that forces you to upgrade or refine a situation that has been outgrown. Uranus is a slow moving planet, giving the intellect time to fully grasp a concept by thinking of ways to slightly improve it or make it work specifically for you. Uranus is here to make our communication exquisite and to jolt us into actions that benefit the whole. Lets take a deep breath in for the Uranus and hold the breath, 5, 4, 3, 2, 1, and exhale allowing the thoughts in you mind to soften to soften. REPEAT: "Uranus, please help me see the path as I remove my personal motivations to the side ", inhale deeply, exhale completely and soften the tension around your jaw and in your mouth.

Lastly we will focus on the outermost planet of the solar system, Neptune. Another gaseous planet, it lies on the exterior realms of the galaxy, but represents the exterior realms of our mind. Neptune gives us the focus to see outside of our reality and extends to realities that encompass us all as one, not separate. Neptune shows us where our talents lie and how we can best serve the collective consciousness. It is the planet that represents overall happiness in life and the meaningful steps to get there. Lets take a deep breath in for the Neptune and hold the breath, 5, 4, 3, 2, 1, and exhale allowing the thoughts in you mind to soften to soften. REPEAT: "Neptune, please show me how to best serve the world and myself for ultimate happiness ", inhale deeply, exhale completely, and so It is.

A MEDITATION FOR THOSE WHO HAVE PASSED ON
This meditation is a loving tribute to the people you love dearly that have departed the earth or are anticipated to leave soon. Before closing your eyes, remember that you are loved, safe and the emotions that come into your awareness are merely there to help you see how important your connection truly was. If you have any photos or mementos you'd like to set out for this meditation, now is the time. Sit in a position you enjoy being in whether its correct posture or not. Please close your eyes and inhale as an image of the person you love so much comes into your awareness, tell them hi as they show you what it is they would like for you to remember, not the images of pain, but the images of joy. Recollect a memory you feel was most enjoyable between the two of you and engage deeply. Take in any nostalgic smells or tastes that

come to mind as you spend time with your dearly departed. Now is the time to tell them something you haven't had the chance to say, what is it? Go ahead and speak it out loud and when you are finished take a long deep inhale and hold the breath, 5, 4, 3, 2, 1, exhale out with an open mouth. Again inhale and hold the breath, 5, 4, 3, 2, 1, dramatically exhale out with an open mouth. REPEAT: "I honor you in my practice today as I remember all the beautiful times we've shared together. While not perfect, I cherish what we had and I thank you for being in my life", inhale deeply, exhale completely, and so It is.

A MEDITATION FOR STRENGTH IN RELATIONSHIPS
This meditation is for those who feel the need to improve the dynamic in the relationships they belong to, whether it be friendship, romantic or familial, we play an important roll in each one and this meditation is to help bring more to the table for each one. Please find a comfortable seated position that is free from interruption. Close your eyes and begin taking long deep inhale's and exhale's as you center yourself, with each inhale you feel your body expand, and with each exhale you sink deeper into your body, noticing each subtle feeling of comfort achieved. You will now visualize the person you'd like to strengthen a relationship with keep the image of them in your head as you recollect why you feel it needs work, think back to the situations that made it apparent your relationship needs elevation.

As your mind scans to any images that are unsavory or memories that make you feel heated, take a deep inhale and slowly exhale– breath through any painful moments as you take full stock of your connection, its importance, and the reason you are sitting here today. Slow the mind down a bit as you remove your concentration from the person and direct your attention to your heart. Visualize a small plant growing at the base of your heart, take a moment to water it and watch it grow. REPEAT: "I love you with all of your imperfections and I know you love me for mine, that is what makes this a divine connection". Take a long deep inhale and hold the breath, 5, 4, 3, 2, 1, exhale as slowly as you can. Again, inhale and hold the breath, 5, 4, 3, 2, 1, and exhale the breath making a hissing sound with the mouth.

AN AFFIRMATION TO SELF-DEVELOPMENT
I honor the process I find myself in today as I realize there is more I'd like to feel from within. My experience does not revolve around external gratification, but one of internal satisfaction and delicate focus towards my bright and expansive future. I imagine who I will be once I am complete and polished, knowing deep down however, I never will be, I wonder where my life will decide to turn next? As I implement small incremental changes, I notice the distance I've gone to get to this place– a long road and there is no turning back. Self development is more than a diet or morning routine

that touts a perfect life, its developing one's emotional and mental state so it is prepared for chaos should it ensue. Its putting the steps in place so I continue to rise. While learning new processes, I find out which one looks best on me, I don't follow dogma or the paths of other people, I follow my own unique process.

A MEDITATION FOR BALANCE

Please sit a comfortable seated position and close your eyes. We are working on balance— balance towards where our energy and mental faculties are spent. With your eyes closed, begin to visualize a scale, its gold with a sturdy base and two large plates, one on each side. Imagine putting all of your our goals, aspirations and hopes for the future on one side of the scale, what happens? If we take a full experience, from beginning to end by interpreting its reality to be a bad one and put experience on one side of the scale, nothing else, where would you find yourself? Take into your minds eye that the scale must constantly move on each side. One will become heavier than the other weighing it down and showing its impact so that you will easily notice when more needs to be added to the other side. Keep watching the scales move up and down evenly— this is a representation of the duality or polarity of life. When we absorb both sides we get the highest expression to come forth. Taking the example above as a positive, but uncomfortable experience even though plans fell through or chaos ensued, we have to come to grips that more occurred out of that experience, something that is to be learned from or harnessed for strength. Take a long deep inhale and hold the breath, repeat the word *balance 3 times,* and exhale as slowly as you can. Again, inhale and hold the breath, 5, 4, 3, 2, 1, and exhale completely. And so it is.

AN AFFIRMATION FOR THE KUNDALINI

Today I honor the 7 energy centers in my body because I am fully aware of what they're about, where they are located in my body and what they are meant to do for me. My root chakra supports the base of my body where it all begins, helping me release my mental blockages around the past and where Im meant to be. My sacral chakra gives my body balance through aligning with my sexuality. It is here where my digestion gives me a head start, not only do I process the nutrients of my body here, but this is where my mental digestion starts to take place, where I begin to understand where I was and where I am headed. My solar plexus chakra aids in the breath given to life, it is where Prana and Apana live– the inhale and the exhale. When the breath is followed, listened for, and cultivated life blooms. Creation manifests as completed goals, creative self expression, and confidence. Projection is made here. My heart chakra keeps me open and vulnerable, ready to display the capacity to let go and allow someone to know me, so they may learn how to love me. My throat chakra controls my voice and contribution in physical form. It is where my authenticity shines through and I express who "self" is to others. I speak my peace and give others an ear. This is the place I hear. My third eye is a special place, it is the eye that sees behind the eyelids when closed. It is where my sense of direction comes from and where my intuition is acted out. I see beyond what my two eyes see, I see who I am on the inside. My crown chakra is where I receive the messages from the outer world to complete my inner world. It is the place where no thinking happens, no knowing happens, no-thing happens— its where I go to "be". All of my chakras work together to make me a whole human being with the desire to expand my consciousness. Awakening the Kundalini awakens my consciousness and opens the world as I know it to states I could never dream of achieving. I was made for this journey and the journey is mine.

AN AFFIRMATION FOR MOTIVATION

I am a strong, motivated person, what gets me moving in life is the promise of something more. Motivation comes when work is to be done, when my heart is truly in it and a sense of purpose has been understood. I realize there are times of rest and I cannot mistake these times for being unmotivated, these are times of rest and processing. However, when I'm done putting together my plan and I let go of judging my progress, I am propelled forward. Getting off the couch is much easier now because the light is showing brightly at the end of the tunnel. I am ready to walk into the life I dream of everyday. As I sit in places I'd rather not be, I gestate my passion in life and turn it into aspiration. I am not limited by my circumstances, I am limited by the capacity to see my freedom. The less I tie myself to material objects or specific places to be, the more freedom I achieve. Freedom is truly endless opportunity of choice. I'm able to choose any direction, you are free. I am motivated by my freedom, my limitless ability to move around the world and the endless experiences I am meant to have.

A MEDITATION FOR SELF CONFIDENCE

This meditation is to shine a light on the larger meanings to not feeling confident with who you are. Identifying when it is felt, what it looks like, and when it crops up are all a part of getting to higher states of emotional intelligence. As you think about yourself as a unique individual with a set of fingerprints all your own, DNA that could never be replicated and an expression that could not be replicated even if you were born on the same day, you start to realize that your whole life experience is one of sovereignty. Your life is not signified by how similar you can make yourself be to other people. Its true that being authentic and confident feels like a risk, it can be a risk of not wanting to be rejected or possessing large amounts of fear around not being accepted or received. The idea is not to change exactly who you are at this moment, but instead to take small steps towards opening up to your confident life expression. It takes people a long time to develop certain unwanted habits and for some, it may take just as long to change them. Where you fall is unique for your life and for a brief moment in this meditation you will get a chance to uplift your confidence.

In a comfortable seated position, straighten your back by arching it slightly and lifting your chest high, roll your neck to get some flexibility in the shoulders. Be sure your sit bones are firmly planted, don't be afraid to move and lift the flesh around your thighs to make sure you feel firmly planted. Place the backs of your hands on the tops of your thighs, palms to the sky as you put your hands in Gian Mudra. First finger and thumb will touch at the tips making a zero while the other fingers stick out straight in front of them, stacked together. Take three long deep breaths, each one bringing you deeper into your body, each one relieving tension in the chest and back. Check your posture again, back straight, chest up, and chin slightly tucked in.

Bring your awareness situation that left you in a state of not feeling confident. What were you doing and what were you trying to accomplish at that moment? Is there a logical explanation to why you don't feel confident? Take a deep inhale 3, 2, 1, and exhale slowly. Take your attention away from what doesn't make you feel confident and instead put your focus towards what does. What are you wearing when you walk in your essence? Visualize yourself walking down the street with your head held high, wearing your most prized possessions, feeling healthy and on track with your routines and excited for where your adventure will land you for the day. You don't have a care in the world because you are not concerned with anything anyone thinks about you. When people say hello as they pass you, you warmly show all teeth and grin and reply with an exuberant "hello, have a great day". You exude what it means to be a present and engaged with life, prepared to take on challenge and chaos should it show its ugly head. AND SO IT IS.

A MEDITATION FOR BEING IN THE PLACE YOU'RE MEANT TO BE

This is a meditation to imagine where in the world you should be. Are you wondering if there is somewhere else you'd like to live or work? Is there a location in your minds eye that represents what it means to be in paradise and what is paradise to you? In a comfortable seated position, straighten your back by arching it slightly and lifting your chest high, roll your neck to get some flexibility in the shoulders. Be sure your sit bones are firmly planted, don't be afraid to move and lift the flesh around your thighs to make sure you feel firmly planted. Place the backs of your hands on the tops of your thighs, palms to the sky as you put your hands in

Gian Mudra. First finger and thumb will touch at the tips making a zero while the other fingers stick out straight in front of them, stacked together. Take three long deep breaths, each one bringing you deeper into your body, each one relieving tension in the chest and back. Check your posture again, back straight, chest up, and chin slightly tucked in.

Bring your awareness to the first place your mind focuses on that to you, represents your sense of freedom, the place the brings you the greatest joy when you lay your eyes upon it. Now that you see the place, lets expand on it some more. Inhale deeply, exhale completely. What are the colors you witness in your visualization? Is there a color that sticks out to you the most? Would it happen to match any of your chakra centers? If this vision takes place outside, focus on what the weather like and how does it feels on your skin. Look up, take view of the sky and its movements. If this vision takes place inside, what is the temperature of the room and are you comfortable? Take a seat next to the nearest window and look up to take a view of the sky and what moves above your head. Imagine what your life would look like in this space all the time, living and breathing in your idea of paradise. Take a moment to go through your regular routine in this space and if you need to adjust what you do for a living to make it work to your advantage. What kinds of foods are at your disposal for nourishment? Are there activities you can enroll your self in or communities you can join? Who is living next to you and how do you interact with each other? Think about how you will effect change in this new place and the people you will come across. Consider the new or expanded love within your relationships and being in love with your life. Take a long deep inhale and hold the breath, REPEAT the words *"everyday I get closer to paradise"* *3 times,* and exhale as slowly as you can. Again, inhale and hold the breath, 5, 4, 3, 2, 1, and exhale completely. And so it is.

AN AFFIRMATION TO TRY ON A NEW MENTAL SPACE

When you go for coffee, or stop for groceries, take a moment to smile - even if that isn't how you feel on the inside. When you walk into a building - hold the door for the next person with that same smile. Initially your actions may not be met in the way you'd like, people are moving through the world with their own worries. The goal of the game is to enjoy the act of smiling regardless of how others respond until eventually your energy becomes infectious and you are met with smiles and gratitude in return!

A MEDITATION ON MINDFULNESS

Still your body. Allow our mind to wander. In most meditation practices we work to allow our thoughts to float by with non attachment. With this meditation we want to take notice of where our thoughts go and how they make us feel. Do you feel happy, energized and uplifted? Our mind feeds us thoughts on repeat, and like outdated files they must eventually be overwritten. Pick an unwanted thought or image when it comes up and immediately try to think of something that brings you joy. With practice we can change the trajectory of our most destructive thought processes, overwriting destructive data.

Lightning Source UK Ltd.
Milton Keynes UK
UKHW021839200622
404701UK00009B/1564